GEORGIAN
HOUSES
FOR ALL

FRONTISPIECE   A regency pair in Bath, designed with a unifying
pediment to look like one villa: each semi-detached house has its
entrance in a small side wing. The central windows of the façade
never had a practical purpose and the original paintwork simulating
panes of glass can still be seen. An occupant of the right-hand house
has had the windows bisected in the uneasy Victorian manner.

GEORGIAN HOUSES FOR ALL

JOHN WOODFORDE

Routledge & Kegan Paul
London, Boston, Melbourne and Henley

Also by John Woodforde

The Strange Story of False Teeth
The Truth about Cottages
The Story of the Bicycle
The Strange Story of False Hair
Bricks to Build a House

First published in 1978
First published as a paperback in 1985
by Routledge & Kegan Paul plc
14 Leicester Square, London WC2H 7PH,
9 Park Street, Boston, Mass., 02108, USA,
464 St Kilda Road, Melbourne,
Victoria 3004, Australia and
Broadway House, Newtown Road,
Henley-on-Thames, Oxon RG9 1EN
Set in Monophoto Baskerville
and printed in Great Britain by
St Edmundsbury Press,
Bury St Edmunds, Suffolk
© John Woodforde 1978

British Library Cataloguing in Publication Data

Woodforde, John
  Georgian houses for all.
  1. Architecture, Domestic – Great Britain – History
  2. Architecture, Georgian
  I. Title
  728'.0941   NA7328   77-30310
ISBN 0 7100 8680 6 (c)
ISBN 0 7102 05236 (p)

CONTENTS

AUTHOR'S NOTE   xiv

I   PALLADIAN COMFORT   I

*Over a million Georgian houses still in existence – symmetry meeting a need for
reassurance – eighteenth-century escape from brutality – a willingness to live in
identical terrace houses – the compulsion to make old houses appear classical and
modern – builders who followed Palladio more closely than they knew –
elegance and neatness with mud*

2   FIVE TYPES OF HOUSE   I I

*Detached and terrace – the gradual disappearance of regional variations –
English dormer windows imposed on classical fronts – the ideal of four rooms to
a floor – metropolitan houses in the country – the pretext for basements and for
ponds – fifth to fourth rate houses in London – the main characteristics of Queen
Anne, early Georgian, mid-Georgian and late Georgian houses, with hints on
dating*

3   **BUILDERS AND LANDLORDS I**   25

The craftsman builders – the wide variety of people undertaking to build houses – subcontracting – pattern books by and for craftsmen – organizing house building in the industrial towns – how building speculators worked in London – carpenters who became master builders and architects – contemporary concern about ill-built houses – effects of the great London Building Act of 1774

4   **BUILDERS AND LANDLORDS II**   33

Staking out the ground – high potential rewards for landowners – covenants for controlling the appearance of houses – achieving a select town estate – financial risks for developers – the first modern building firm – house ownership as an investment

5   **THE FIRST TERRACE HOUSES**   40

Nicholas Barbon 'casting ground into streets' – thick walls of brick stipulated for London after the Great Fire – mass-production of panelling and balusters for terrace houses – economies in brickwork and the use of fake Flemish bond – footings of wood which have left trouble for posterity – bonding timbers leading to distortion of walls – the setting back of window frames as a fire precaution – an early eighteenth-century enthusiasm for Palladio and its effect on the terrace house

6   **LIVING IN LONDON**   49

Thomas Carlyle's house – where servants slept – the air of Chelsea vibrating with noise – street dangers in London and their effect on house construction – the London house compared to a birdcage – intermittent water supplied by wooden pipes – life in the elegant squares

7   **BUILDING MATERIALS AND ECONOMY**   58

Use of household waste in brickmaking – London stock bricks and how they were made – houses built with unfired earth – cheap mortar – economies in various building materials – thin walls – the original purpose of stucco – the economies of Nash – the brick tax – a shortage of brick earth in the industrial towns – house prices reduced in Birmingham – dancing forbidden in the upper rooms of certain houses – floors under-ceiled to hide softwood joists and rough work

8   THE FARMHOUSE   64

*The effect of classical farmhouses on farmers – the villa farmhouse – farmhouse
front doors less elegant than those of parsonages – farm servants unable to live-
in – abandoned village-street farmhouses serving as cottages – contemporary
views on the manners of farmers with a taste for show – accommodation of
married farm servants – John Wood junior on farm cottages – American
farmhouses*

9   THE PARSONAGE   76

*Cottage status of the majority of parsonages – model designs for parsonages –
the period before it was decided that God preferred the Gothic style – parsons in
easy circumstances not squeamish about display – hints taken from Palladian
mansions – family livings – a contemporary's comments about money spent on a
parsonage rather than on a roofless church – the growth in size of studies – a
parson driven to dissipation through lack of a study – the effect of pluralism – a
mania for building among Regency clergymen – the clergy metaphorically
seeking lost sheep but no longer farming*

10   FURNISHING AND LIGHTING   85

*Drawbacks to the compact plan of a small Georgian house – sparse furnishings
– the hanging of pictures – mirrors – hardly any household object ill-formed –
housework – a distaste for antiques – the spread of fashions downward from
London – the continuing use of walnut, despite mahogany – a description of
changes in furnishing in Bath – a demand for china ornaments – the importance
of candles – getting a light from tinder boxes*

11   BEDROOMS   98

*Sleeping in a draught-free cabin – steps for getting into it – four-post and tent
beds – ways of cleaning beds – a bed-bug destroyer to the queen – the smallness
of early wash basins – having a bath considered eccentric – crockery for the
bedroom and the two meanings of chamber and commode*

12   # HYGIENE   104

Jonathan Swift on sanitary arrangements – throwing rubbish from windows – necessary houses – an accident with sewer gas – the night men – a waste material of use to farmers – contaminated drinking water – water closets – the lack of ventilation pipes – mains water – limited uses for soap – kitchens – the first local authorities and their effect on hygiene – the rising birth rate of the 1790s

13   # THE SASH WINDOW   111

Sliding sash versus hinged casement – disadvantages of casement windows – their origin and development – Samuel Johnson on sash windows in the Hebrides – an accident with a falling sash described by Sterne – the proportions for sash windows – how the glass was made – shop windows – the window tax – blocked windows – new placings for window openings in the Regency – the continuing merits of sliding sashes

14   # CHIMNEYS AND FIREPLACES   121

Chimney pots a Georgian invention – a case for removing them – invisible chimney pots – the Georgians' lack of interest in chimney construction – problems over inventing a classical fireplace – changing fashions in surrounds and grates – the use of artificial marble – influence of open fires on furniture design – the birth of the kitchen range

15   # NON-CLASSICAL WORK   129

Scattered attempts to break away from a universal style – playfully-Gothic houses – Gothic fireplaces and beds – the Chinese taste – Walpole's Strawberry Hill and its influence – the pull of the Middle Ages – witticisms about the new roadside retreats – a new Gothic castle and Gothic cottage on the Isle of Wight – Regency Gothic and the Greek revival – the approach of the Battle of the Styles

16 THE VILLAS AND THE END 140

*The range from rich men's secondary seats to Jubilee Villas – villas by Nash –
a preoccupation among young architects from the end of the eighteenth century –
cottage ornée often an appropriate label – hilltop sites – Jane Austen's
comments on 'stareabouts' – beginning of the end of the Renaissance-Palladian
manner – Howitt's comments on house snobs in the country – houses in pairs
carefully designed to appear one house – suburban villas more interesting in the
provinces than in London – characteristics of Regency domestic architecture,
with hints on dating*

17 ARCHIVAL RECORDS 152

*The main repositories – documents to look for – information more likely to be
found about farmhouses and parsonages than about other small houses –
contemporary drawings of houses on estate maps – surveys, probate inventories
and estimates – examples of information that may be available – deductions to
be made from this – the lack of documented history concerning individual
cottages*

18 THE GEORGIAN TRADITION REVIVED 162

*Beginnings of a revival around the year 1900 – neo-Georgianism – use of the
classical language of architecture by Raymond Erith – adjustment and invention
in the classical tradition – the planners now readier to approve – present-day use
of the works of Palladio – the efforts of modernists to stop avoiding traditional
forms and methods*

BIBLIOGRAPHY 168

INDEX 171

ILLUSTRATIONS

Regency semi-detached houses: photograph by
author   *frontispiece*

1 A child's drawing which shows an instinct for
  symmetry and for the Georgian box shape   2
2 Dignity and order in a classical house: Mary
  Evans Picture Library   3
3 Palladian mansion   5
4 Easy-to-climb staircase: Mary Evans Picture
  Library   6
5 A Palladian house by Palladio: courtesy of Mr
  James S. Ackerman, *Palladio*, Penguin, 1966   7
6 Mid-Georgian house: courtesy of the estate of the
  late Harry Forrester and Tindal Press, publishers
  of his book *The Smaller Queen Anne and Georgian
  House*, 1964   9
7 Two-room plan   12
8 Four-room plans   13
9 Queen Anne roofs: Harry Forrester   14
10 Elevations for houses of four rooms to a floor:
   Harry Forrester   14

11	Elevation for a house of two rooms to a floor: Harry Forrester	16
12	Queen Anne front doors: Harry Forrester	18
13	Early Georgian doorcase: Harry Forrester	19
14	Further early Georgian doorcases: Harry Forrester	20
15	Mid-Georgian doorcase: Harry Forrester	21
16	Late Georgian doorcase: Harry Forrester	23
17	Doorcase in a contemporary pattern book: courtesy of Mr Dan Cruikshank	28
18	Small village-street house	36
19	Adam motifs: Harry Forrester	38
20	Plan of an early terrace house	41
21	The Fire of London: courtesy of Weinreb & Dowma Ltd, their catalogue *Plans of London*, 1968	43
22	Sixteenth-century street house in Rome: courtesy of Mr James S. Ackerman, *Palladio*, Penguin, 1966	45
23	A London terrace: Harry Forrester	46
24	Plan of L-shaped terrace house	47
25	Wall panelling: Harry Forrester	51
26	Street vendors in London: courtesy of Pollock's Toy Theatres Ltd	52
27	Knife grinder: courtesy of Pollock's Toy Theatres Ltd	53
28	Wigs as part of the striving for order: Mary Evans Picture Library	56
29	Bricklaying: Harry Forrester	61
30	Bonfires to encourage mortar to set	62
31	Scene of gluttony: courtesy of BBC Publications	66
32	Typical eighteenth-century farmhouse: courtesy of Mr S. R. Badmin, *Village and Town*, Penguin, c. 1948	67
33	Plan of seventeenth-century farmhouse	69
34	Model semi-detached cottages	71
35	A North American farmhouse	74
36	A parson by his fireside: Radio Times Hulton Picture Library	79

37 A parson being waited on: Radio Times Hulton
    Picture Library   81
38 A parson making notes: Radio Times Hulton
    Picture Library   83
39 Lack of space in the dining room   87
40 Pleasing design of everyday objects: Radio Times
    Hulton Picture Library   89
41 A drawing room: Radio Times Hulton Picture
    Library   91
42 Regency furniture in use: Abbot Hall Art Gallery,
    Kendal   95
43 A candle for four: Abbot Hall Art Gallery,
    Kendal   96
44 Four-post bed: courtesy of Warne, *The Observer's
    Book of Furniture*   100
45 Pre-Georgian windows: Harry Forrester; upper
    drawing, courtesy of Mr David Iredale, *This Old
    House*, Shire Publications   112
46 A classical and a Gothic window: Harry Forrester   113
47 Details of early sash window: Harry Forrester   115
48 Late Georgian windows: Harry Forrester   117
49 Chimney development: courtesy of Mr David
    Ireland, *This Old House*, Shire Publications   123
50 Queen Anne fireplace: Harry Forrester   124
51 Early Georgian fireplaces: Harry Forrester   125
52 Mid-Georgian fireplaces: Harry Forrester   126
53 Hob grates: Harry Forrester   127
54 Regency fireplace: Harry Forrester   128
55 Classical small house   131
56 Gothic small house   133
57 Garden temple in the Chinese style: courtesy of
    The Royal Institute of British Architects   134
58 A Gothic library: Radio Times Hulton Picture
    Library   136
59 Regency Gothic house: courtesy of British
    Architectural Library   137

60 Georgian Gothic porch: Harry Forrester   138
61 A Palladian villa by Palladio: courtesy of Mr
    James S. Ackerman, *Palladio*, Penguin, 1966   141
62 Regency villa: Harry Forrester   143
63 Greek Doric portico: Harry Forrester   145
64 Greek Doric doorcase: Harry Forrester   146
65 Details of Regency roofs: Harry Forrester   148
66 Regency external cornices: Harry Forrester   149
67 The classical orders of architecture: Harry
    Forrester   150
68 Builder's design for a farmhouse: courtesy of Miss
    Nancy Briggs, *Georgian Essex*, Essex County
    Council, 1968   154
69 Small classical cottages   160
70 A Georgian house modernized in 1930s style:
    courtesy of the Greater London Council, *Do You
    Care about Historic Buildings?*   164
71 The Georgian manner revived: courtesy of the
    firm of architects, Erith and Terry, Dedham,
    Essex   166

AUTHOR'S NOTE

I want to thank four distinguished members of the Council of the Georgian Group for supplying a rough personal estimate of the number of small Georgian houses built before 1830 and still in position. Their guesses, with mine, give a joint guess of 1,100,000. Even if the figure should be too high by several hundred thousand (it could be too low), it probably still represents more houses of the period than in any other country regardless of size: China is immense, but the wooden houses were built for eventual replacement. A difficulty in attempting an estimate is produced by the number of non-Georgian houses which grace town streets in Georgian-fronted form.

I am grateful, as usual, to the London Library, where the opportunity to browse anywhere often yields source books one would not have thought of asking for; I am also grateful to Ashford County Library in Kent, and to my wife for her support. No apparatus of notes is offered, at the request of the publisher, sources being indicated in the text.

I

PALLADIAN COMFORT

Ask a child to draw a house and it will almost certainly draw a Georgian house. Even if it lives in a tower block. There will be a door in the middle, a window on each side of this, three windows above and a hipped roof. A symmetrical arrangement of the kind appears to be instinctive; and no other was considered for the houses of the classical, Italian Renaissance style, inspired by Palladio, which in Georgian Britain became universal.

Just over a million small Georgian houses, built in the full period 1700–1830, are believed still to survive in the British Isles. The much greater number existing 200 years ago reflected the fact that by the 1750s an influential middle class far exceeded in numbers any Continental middle class. Its members liked to be occupants of small, trim, classical houses. Without the temperament or wealth to emulate the carefree and often graceless behaviour of the aristocracy, yet anxious to distinguish themselves sharply from the labouring classes, what these people of middle rank especially valued was a degree of dignity and order, a respectable house suggesting some control over nature

1 An instinct for symmetry and for the Georgian box shape seems to come out in this scribble of a child aged seven (she does not live in a Georgian house) when asked to draw a house.

2 Dignity and order in a small classical house, 1783.

and aloofness from all that was brutal and irregular. The symmetrical wigs of horsehair worn by the men were only another symptom of the concern for a limited sphere of order.

Palladian mansions provided the example for small houses, and building craftsmen, copying one another and using pattern books, produced with ease the standard symmetrical houses with a pedimented door that was required. They were the nation's middling houses, in the phrase of Horace Walpole, who said that like the population of 'middling people', they were peculiar to England: France, said Samuel Johnson, had 'no happy middle state'. Such houses, with their graceful restraint, have always tended to flatter their occupants, and in doing this they faithfully interpret Palladio's precepts on human dignity. In one sense they are even more Palladian than the great houses: they are comfortable to live in. Andrea Palladio in the sixteenth century had improved on ancient Greek and Roman work by concentrating as much on human convenience as on pleasure to the eye, and he wrote in *Quattro Libri dell'Architettura*: 'Relate everything in a house to the human frame.'

It certainly cannot be said that the Palladian mansions of England inspired by this book (it was translated in 1676) were built to be inhabited in comfort: their function was to look magnificent, and to be approached from an angle to appear at their grandest. The coldness of the large rooms and galleries in part explains the delight of the aristocracy with seaside lodgings and their little rooms. A letter by Lady Sarah Spencer (quoted in Betty Askwith's *The Lytteltons*), makes it clear that the delicious warmth and convenience of a small house which her family took in Ryde outweighed the inconvenience of being 'surrounded by pigsties, butchers' shops, ill-covered sewers, drunken sailors and noisy children'.

But the feeling of comfort came from more than small rooms. The builders, as they executed their compact, standard designs, considered human convenience in a way which Palladio would have approved. Their staircases, for instance, met his suggestions in being easy to climb and having a baluster rail so shaped that it was inviting to the hand. The size of the human frame was taken

3 Palladian mansion by Colen Campbell, c. 1715, with its owners:
Wanstead House, Essex, demolished 1822.

into account in all parts of a house. If today we must stoop at a
lintel, that is because the human frame has got bigger.

The good-mannered house-fronts fit in with Palladio's view
that architecture should enhance people's dignity: don't let them
be confused or belittled, show clearly where the entrance is.
Small Georgian houses never lack an easily seen, graceful front
door. Palladio advised builders to place all doorways in such a
way that 'one may see from one end of the house to the other', for
this was 'at all times graceful and in summer cool'. To open the
front door of almost any Georgian house, detached or joined to
others, is to expose a vista right through it to light and greenery
beyond.

Even Britain's wealth of town gardens made comfortable with
high brick walls seem to owe something to Palladio. He strongly
recommended the private court. The French in general ignored
his precepts, and few who live in central Paris have anywhere to
grow things. I used to have a simple Georgian terrace house in
London and one summer afternoon heard an excited comment
by a French woman who had been glancing through my open
front door. 'Do look', she cried to a companion. 'They even have
large gardens at the back.'

4 Easy-to-climb staircase for a big Palladian house which has Venetian windows. The letters of identification are concerned with perspective. From a pattern book of 1775.

6

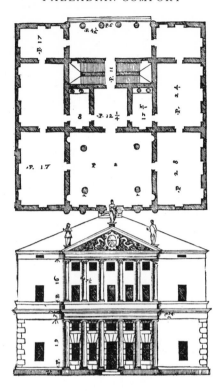

5   A Palladian house by Palladio, 1556. It is the Palazzo Antonini
which may still be seen at Udine, Italy, where it was designed for a
narrow street. The central pedimented portico, with pillars on both
storeys, contrasts with very simple flanking wings. From Andrea
Palladio, *Quattro Libri*.

The mere outward appearance of small classical houses was so appealing that those without one felt a sense, peculiar to the eighteenth century, of being architecturally deprived and unfashionable. During the nineteenth century people came to admire something quite different, but few thought it shameful to live in a Tudor or Georgian house: in towns prosperous during Georgian times, like Bury St Edmunds and Chichester, those who found themselves still in old timber-framed houses can have scarcely cared to show their faces.

In market towns all over England street after street became classical, sometimes by demolition and re-building but more often by covering over and by the addition of a parapet. The great aim was to banish timber studwork, and no building was too mediaeval for the craftsmen employed to provide a classically-featured façade. Sash windows were forced into position. Perfect symmetry was commonly impossible because of the plan, but the workmen seemed to enjoy doing their best, and their customers modernized their fireplaces and wall coverings.

Several ways of economically re-fronting houses were devised. Brickwork showing Flemish bond was unexceptionable and popular, the brick being only four and a half inches thick and the headers merely half-bricks. In the south-east massive use was made of a brick skin in the form of mathematical tiles which, when nailed on and filled round with mortar, perfectly resembled brickwork, while escaping the tax on bricks imposed in 1784: houses so faced still exist in abundance, especially in Lewes, and demolition men and architects have been known to be deceived.

Although brick was admired, a snobbish craving for the cachet of stone led to the creation of stone effects with other materials. With a timber-framed building the trick was performed cheaply enough with scored plaster or stucco – though when jetties were not obliterated, as at the King's School shop in Palace Street, Canterbury, the effect was disturbing. Stone corner-dressings for brickwork were often successfully simulated with plaster: this had been a device of Palladio's.

In some towns, wood itself, suitably painted, was the material

6 Mid-Georgian house with parapet and tall pilasters (Dedham, Essex), calculated to make those with a less-than-classical house feel deprived.

for making a wooden building appear to be of stone. The cheapest procedure was to face a house with non-overlapping boards and score them vertically at regular intervals to suggest blocks of stone, as on buildings in The Pantiles, Tunbridge Wells and several houses in Tenterden. A slightly better deception was possible with separate rectangles of wood, each carefully chamfered.

Georgian craftsmen became adept enough to create the refined classical look even for the houses being built of unbaked earth; these became more plentiful after a doubling of the brick tax in 1794. The West Country house of cob and straw (laid on wet) may have a chunky, rustic look, but England elsewhere still contains houses of hidden clay lump, or of pisé de terre (dry earth rammed down between shuttering), whose classically modelled rendering makes them Georgian with the best. Earth building by the pisé method actually had a spell of fashionable patronage,

9

thanks to high praise for it by the distinguished architect Henry Holland (he built earth estate houses at Woburn in the 1790s) and by John Plaw, another architect, who seemed to think, in his book *Ferme Ornée* of 1788, that pisé was his own discovery.

If this first chapter has a theme, it is simply that, in the face of an overwhelming fashion, Georgian craftsmen, following Andrea Palladio more closely than they knew, cheerfully learned how to meet it in any material that lay to their hand. Hence the amazingly wide distribution of small Georgian houses which appear, when seen as shapes only, to have come out of the same mould. The watchwords of builders and their clients were two words plentifully used in the eighteenth century, neatness and elegance.

2

FIVE TYPES OF HOUSE

Georgian domestic architecture was the first kind to rise above the regional variations of vernacular building, none of its house-fronts, at least, conforming to any pattern but that of the Italian Renaissance. A classical house of granite in Lancashire looks very much like a classical brick house in Kent, though the first may be seventy-five or more years younger than the second. The new way of building took a long time to reach the north from the more advanced south-east; it did, however, speedily reach Ireland, especially in its purest Palladian form, doing so, as Sir John Summerson has said, as easily as if the Irish Sea were a boundary between two counties.

Behind the family likeness of their classical faces, fitted increasingly with sash windows, small Georgian houses have in the main one of five plans: 1. The cottage type, one room thick, two up and two down. 2. The same with a lean-to extension – all under one roof. 3. L-shaped, the rear wing containing the kitchen. 4. Square with four rooms on each floor: this type, with rooms compactly disposed on each side of the central entrance was the ideal, and best reflects the Italian influence. 5. The single-fronted terrace house.

The only non-classical part of many Georgian houses is the roof, steeply pitched to deal with rain, and its dormer windows. Previously rooms in the roof had been easily lit by windows in the gable ends. Now, even where gable ends had not been hipped

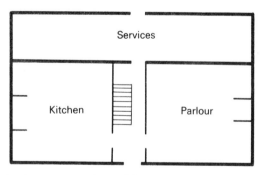

7   A standard two-room plan, with lean-to, used throughout the eighteenth century.

12

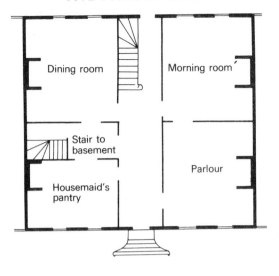

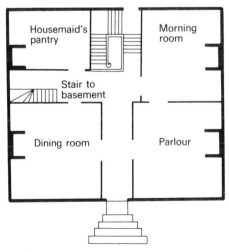

8 Four-room plans standard by the early eighteenth century.

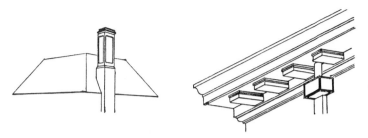

9 Queen Anne roofs. Left: truncated and hipped; recessed panels to chimney stack. Right: Projecting wooden eaves cornice; modillions in the bed mould; rain water gutter, lead-lined, in upper part of cornice.

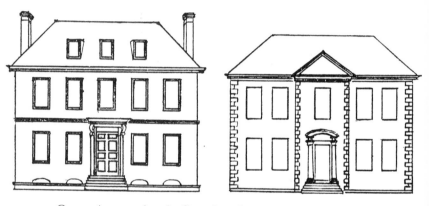

10 Queen Anne and early Georgian elevations for houses having four rooms to a floor. Right: the more-than-ordinary small house which has been furnished with a central pedimented portico and rusticated corner stones.

back, a cornice had often to be considered, and there was a reluctance to break its horizontal line with wall surfaces above. Dormers thus became a necessity where the roof space contained rooms; and they began to receive architectural treatment and to be so arranged that they actually added to the good appearance of classical fronts. The huge and elaborate chimney stack, admired by past generations, became two slight stacks symmetrically disposed.

The first four types of house in the list were almost as suitable as the fifth for neatly building up against one another in a town or village street. It was for this they were first designed, but it was soon noticed that they were equally satisfactory for isolated positions. The distinction between the small town houses and small country houses was almost non-existent in the eighteenth century, and thousands in rural settings had railed-in basement areas which gave them a strangely metropolitan look. The Rev. William Cole in 1756 wrote of 'elegant little houses on every outlet from London' – and compared them with 'the wretched buildings on the roads from Paris' – but they made a target for witticisms by Lord Cork in the *Connoisseur* in 1754:

A little country box you boast,
So neat, 'tis cover'd all with dust . . .
'Tis not the country you must own,
'Tis only London out of town.

John Byng, the diarist, in 1781 tried to dissuade a friend from having an underground kitchen for his new house near Cheltenham, 'there being no reason for it in the country'; but cellars were usually everywhere, often because they seemed to make good use of a crater dug by brickmakers in obtaining their brickmaking clay. Byng might have made a more telling argument with the point that the brickmakers' digging could have helped to create a pleasing pond for the garden – numerous ponds are in fact the result of brickmaking activities.

Individual symmetry was impossible for the narrow houses built all together in a terrace (rather than joined together piecemeal), but the essential balance was recovered by the treatment of the terrace as a whole, especially by giving it a unifying cornice; in later Georgian work a parapet would rise to a pediment over a central pair of houses.

Above the basement kitchen, lit from a pit called an area, the main floor began about two feet above the pavement: the steps needed for reaching this level drew attention, in a way Palladio had suggested, to the front door. The hallway, lit by a fanlight, contained a dog-leg stair with a half-landing at the turn. As in all the small houses, the compact layout had the weakness in an era of abundant hospitality, of lacking one room much bigger than the rest; only occasionally were front and back parlours so prepared at the start that one opened into the other.

In London, as will be shown, terrace houses came to be built in five standard categories, first rate down to fifth rate: these were the categories laid down by the Building Act of 1774, each having its code of structural requirements for foundations and external and party walls. The rest of this chapter consists of a summary of the main changes – most of them in style only – which are exhibited by the small houses of the Georgian period, here taken to include the periods of Queen Anne and the Regency.

11 Queen Anne and early Georgian elevation for a cramped site: a type of house with two rooms to a floor often erected in country towns, front door and stairs occupying the whole of the right-hand side.

THE QUEEN ANNE TYPE (*c.* 1700–20)

A typical detached house has two principal storeys, a basement and a dormered attic. Still largely seventeenth-century in character, it has a well-pitched, hipped, tiled roof forming a truncated pyramid. Chimney stacks have panelled sides. A projecting eaves cornice holds a rain water gutter in its upper part: in London the wooden eaves cornice was prohibited as a fire risk and replaced by a low parapet in brick. Quoins, or angles, are emphasized by the use of different coloured brick or stone. Sash windows – the great new invention – are commonly fitted in front, though hinged iron casements may be still in position at the back. The windows of the main floors are all of the same size. Dormer windows retain casements and leaded lights.

Care and invention was expended on doorways, and many had projecting canopies supported on characteristic brackets, these canopies being either straight or hooded, over pilasters. Lighthearted variations were adopted for canopies; one pleasant idea was to make them so deep and round that the inside could be made to resemble a shell.

The front-door cases of minor houses are usually wooden. A popular form has a pedimented entablature with engaged columns, the composition being based on one of the classical orders of architecture. The Doric order, simpler than the Corinthian and the Ionic, is the one usually employed for small houses of some pretension. In such houses the orders are used with a freedom not permitted for mansions.

Panelling inside is characteristic of early Georgian work. It is less heavily treated than that of the late Stuart period; the panels, though still fielded, are slightly sunk in from the line of the wall and no longer bordered by applied bolection moulding. Georgian panelling remained in fashion for minor houses till shortly after the middle of the century when the tendency was to hang wallpaper. Ceilings are generally plain, though with a cornice. Chimneypieces have pilasters with consoles under the cornice, an arrangement characteristic of the period.

12 Queen Anne front doors are often distinguished from later work by a projecting cornice supported on curved brackets with, below these, pilasters on stumpy pedestals. Above: a shell-hooded canopy. Below: a flat canopy. The fanlight consisting of a rectangular fixed sash is a typical means of lighting the hallway.

The setting out of panels was a matter of rules: about two feet nine inches from the floor runs a three-inch moulded dado rail; above this are tall panels, their width commensurate with the size of the room; below, between the dado rail and the skirting, squat panels are squared up with those above. Each panel is framed in a projecting bolection moulding and the fielded panel is itself raised from the line of the wall.

EARLY GEORGIAN TYPE (*c.* 1720–50)

A parapet is not unusual anywhere for the better class of small house; the hidden line of eaves is marked by a simple cornice adding some definition to the walls. Chimney stacks are rarely within the house, but at each side, two pairs of them for a square house; they are now built within the exterior walls and thus cause fireplaces and chimney breasts to project into rooms – the resultant recessed spaces have never ceased to be used for shelves and cupboards. The full length pilasters on the face of more important houses are occasionally seen on small ones, the point of

13 Early Georgian doorcase with the profile of the columns exaggerated to show a boldly swelling outline. The door itself is characteristically eight-panelled.

14 Further early Georgian doorcases. Based on one of the classical orders, these have a curved or triangular pediment. Left: a rich Corinthian example. Right: an Ionic example. Fanlights are now generally semi-circular.

them being, of course, to create an over-all architectural composition and give an impression of height.

MID-GEORGIAN TYPE (*c.* 1750–85)

Such classical details as pilasters and entablature are rarely seen any longer, although the brief cornice below the parapet remains. Façades are plain expanses relieved only by the windows, by the doorway, and by string courses of slightly projecting flat brickwork which is the same colour as the rest of the walls.

Following a reaction against red brick in London, a lot of houses of all sizes were faced with yellow-brown bricks, but in country towns bright red brick was used for angles and window surrounds. In houses of the earlier part of the period, windows continue to present the whole of their white painted frames and to make a good show with an elegant doorway.

The proportion of the sash windows is beautifully calculated to produce a feeling of rest and dignity. Glazing bars are thinner, but not as thin as they were to become. Six panes to a sash is normal on ground and first floors. In the rather more substantial houses, there are short windows on the ground floor for solidity, very tall windows on the first floor for elegance, slightly shorter ones on the next floor and at the top of the house completely square windows as full-stops to arrest the eye. Georgian designers excelled in such subtleties.

Window glass – as in the earlier houses – has a ripply surface, noticeable when looked at from one side: this is caused by the method of manufacture which entailed blowing glass in circular sheets. There may be a bluish tinge to it. Sash fasteners are now fixed to the meeting rails. The barrel fastener with a spring and a butterfly to help manipulation was one of the earliest; thereafter one patent sash fastener followed another, just as in recent years the minutiae of curtain rods and gliders have seen several changes.

All-over wood panelling was not fitted after about 1760, just a dado of sunken panels of plain boards. Later on, the rail of the dado alone persisted, to protect walls from the effect of chairs being pushed against them. The high fashion was for textiles stretched on frames to be fixed above this rail, but in small houses wallpapers were now increasingly hung, especially in bedrooms. In the absence of panelling, a usual treatment for interior walls was colour-washing – blue was the favoured colour because it made a good background for the brown of mahogany furniture. Staircase balusters became slighter and simpler in outline.

15 Mid-Georgian doorcase with a triangular pediment and broken entablature which neatly enclose the Gothic-influenced fanlight.

LATE GEORGIAN TYPES (*c.* 1780–1810)

Even quite small buildings now follow the modified version of the classical style which was introduced by the two architect brothers Robert and James Adam, of whom Robert was the dominant partner. Their inspiration came from study of the designs of ancient Greece and Rome, rather than from Palladio's interpretations of these.

A peculiar refinement and grace smooths out the Palladian influence and the feeling of its closest adherents that the only proper adornment for buildings, inside and out, ought to be the five grammatical elements comprised in the five orders. Robert Adam accepted the traditional symmetries and proportions but began to treat ornament freely. In *Works in Architecture*, which began to come out in instalments in 1773, he argued that the Romans themselves did not bring temple architecture (i.e. columns) into their houses; and the technique of ornament he introduced appealed to rich Londoners, even if it repelled Sir William Chambers, architect for the highly Palladian Somerset House.

Although the work carried out under the instructions and supervision of the Adam brothers was for the rich, the characteristic treatments were soon copied for small houses. The building trade responded indeed with extraordinary rapidity, helped by firms in a position to mass produce stick-on mouldings. Craftsmen went on expeditions to study the thin graceful embroideries of the Adelphi buildings and the pilastered front of Kenwood. Robert Adam himself made it easy for the ordinary builder to copy – by inventing a composition by means of which ornaments could be formed in moulds and then permanently applied. The Adam revolution showed itself most noticeably in a fashion everywhere for his type of front doorway, fireplace, ceiling and wall frieze.

Adam doorways have engaged columns with glazing bars of cast lead. Balconies are made of cast iron wrought fine like filigree. Windows are taller and have glazing bars that are

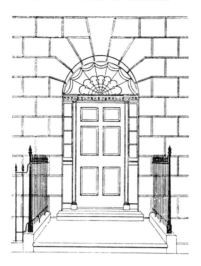

16 Late Georgian doorcase. An Adam type for a town house with its stucco scored, as was usual, to look like stone.

thinner than ever before. Windows with three lights, triple windows, make a feature of quite modest-sized houses; those with a middle light wider than the other two, and arched, are known as Venetian windows. Some houses dating from the close of the century have sash windows of an exaggerated narrowness.

Stucco scored with lines and painted to look like the coveted masonry is often found in houses of the Adam period. This rendering was generally restricted to the ground floor, where it could simulate at trifling cost the rusticated masonry for ground floors of the Palladian houses.

A low dado, painted, is a feature of the best rooms, whether the wall above is decorated or not. Among the Adam ornaments for interior decoration are the anthemion (or Greek honeysuckle) motif, the group of flutes, the wheat-ear, the festoon of wheat-ear and pendants; and for the friezes of chimneypieces and doorcases, the plaque carrying a classical figure or festoon in low relief. Adam schemes of decoration were enhanced by soft shades of colour as refined as the plaster work. The plain plaster walls and ceilings of small houses were commonly given an application of 'Adam' colour-wash.

Many rooms of this period have a curve at one end, or even both ends, this being elliptical or semi-circular; and there are arches and curved niches. This vogue for curved interior walls came to affect the design of even the humblest houses in the Regency period. The characteristics of Regency houses are given at the end of chapter 16.

3

BUILDERS AND LANDLORDS I

In the eighteenth century there were no firms of builders as we know them – that is, firms permanently employing a team of men skilled in a variety of trades. Building craftsmen and labourers were freelances. For a big job a man known as a master builder would gather together the tradesmen needed, and although some of these might be loosely contracted to one another, all enjoyed independence in that they had no regular boss who could dismiss them: a man who fell out with a customer one day might find another to work for the next day.

Occasionally they seemed to overdo their independence of attitude. The Rev. Sydney Smith employed twenty-eight men on re-building a Somerset rectory, that for Combe Florey, and he complained of heavy losses 'through the villainy of bricklayers and carpenters' when he was away for a day or two – even when he was there some came to work already drunk on the local cider.

Smith called himself 'my own architect and clerk of works'. He was in fact a builder (non-profitmaking) in the eighteenth-century sense of one who undertakes a building project and is responsible for all business transactions to do with it. This was a role taken up by all kinds of people; some were well-off members of the professional classes and did not themselves handle a brick, but the majority were bricklayers, carpenters, plumbers and glaziers who had turned master builders and badly needed to make a profit.

The diversity of those whose initiative led to the building of England's small Georgian houses is illustrated by the records of Birmingham, where the stock of houses rose in the period 1746–80 from about 3,000 to about 8,000. In his book *The Provincial Towns of England*, C. W. Chalkin shows that out of 132 builders who were lessees of sites on the Colemore Estate in Birmingham, fifty-six were in the metal trades and twenty-six included several toy makers, five ladies, four gentlemen, a surgeon, a stationer and a clergyman; the remaining fifty were building craftsmen. In the period 1780–1820 the building craftsmen were less prominent and the people who built Bartholomew Street, Birmingham, included six brass founders, two button makers, an engraver, a butcher, a baker, a publican and various women. The range of occupations was similar among the builders of Georgian Nottingham and Manchester, though with the textile rather than the metal trades well represented. A lace manufacturer, two framework knitters, two tailors and a cordwainer built houses in Nottingham's Panier Close.

Building houses was often no more a full-time occupation for the building craftsmen than for 'white-collar' builders outside the trade. Building craftsmen who were prepared to build houses carried out repairs between whiles and helped workmen friends. A few were dealers. Mr Chalkin refers to a Birmingham carpenter – he undertook two large building projects between 1767 and 1771 – who opened a timber yard and in July 1769 advertised in *Aris's Birmingham Gazette*:

> Josiah Deeley, carpenter and joiner, takes this method to inform the public, that he has opened a timber yard opposite the Verulam Printing House in Great Charles Street, Birmingham, where Gentlemen and Tradesmen may be supplied with the following articles upon the most reasonable terms, viz. Building Timber of all Sorts; English and American Oak Boards and Planks; yellow and white Deal, and Packing Boards; he likewise has to dispose of a quantity of 2 inch walnut plank and barrel staves.

A stonemason of Hull, Appleton Bennison, in 1801 advertised in the *Hull Advertiser* three houses which he had built and also

> PLANS and ELEVATIONS drawn at the shortest notice; MARBLE CHIMNEY PIECES and MONUMENTS, executed in the neatest manner.

Because of their skills and experience, ambitious craftsmen, mostly bricklayers and carpenters, found it tempting to build on their own account, the return on let houses in the industrial towns being between 7 and 12 per cent gross. But they were often restricted by lack of capital or credit (except during a period of credit expansion in the early 1790s), and had to fall back on sub-contract work – where at least payment was forthcoming during or immediately after completion of the job. A few became

prosperous. But the typical craftsman house-builder jogged along, mixing the occasional speculation with contract and repair work; he could confidently call himself a master builder when he had satisfactorily handled the construction of his first whole house on speculation. Such a man, capable of attracting a gang of skilled workmen, was the obvious type for a building undertaker without knowledge of the trade to seek as an ally.

To set up as a master builder a man needed £100 capital, it was said; in practice bricklayers and carpenters with only a pound or two in their pockets entered the speculative business, and many such failed. Craftsmen figure prominently in the bankruptcy lists of the eighteenth century.

Nearly all the houses for Georgian London were speculations. The person who had acquired a site, and arranged matters, just went ahead building, hoping that customers would in due course come forward. His technique, adopted more or less in other towns, was this: he signed a building agreement with the owner of the land, taking a 60 or perhaps 90-year lease, and for the first year was charged a peppercorn rent. (In the provinces no rent at all might be asked for during construction, and in some localities leases ran for 999 years.)

During that initial period he worked hard to erect the shells of

17 A doorcase in a contemporary pattern book where Georgian carpenters would have been expected to follow these instructions: 'Doric front drawn half an inch to a foot: the clear passage 3 feet 6 inches, the height 7 feet 2 inches, to be divided into nine equal parts, one of which parts will be the diameter of the column at bottom; give one of them to the sub-plinth, half a one to the base, half a one to the cap of the column, and two to the entablature, that will be 30 minutes to the entablature, 45 minutes to the frieze, and 45 minutes to the cornice; the distance from centre to centre of the column is 6 diameters 15 minutes, which will take 5 modillions; to find the pitch of the pediment set the compass at *a* in the tympan of the pediment, and draw the circle *b, c, a*, then set the compass at *c* and draw the arch *b, d, e*, which gives the height of the pediment at *d*; this method will give the pitch of any pediment.' From William Pain, *The Practical House Carpenter*, 1789.

as many houses as he could, with floors and roof, and advertised a long lease. He might be so lucky as to find a purchaser before the peppercorn rent period expired and thus have no ground rent to pay. The customer would take the house, finished and equipped to his taste, for a lump sum, with the lease made out in his name. Thus the land the builder built on merely passed through the builder's hands. The actual owner of the land rarely erected houses on it.

In London, a town very much larger than any other, the building trade had an exceptional amount of skills to call on. The craftsmen well-trained in a variety of different crafts – the carpenters, joiners, masons, bricklayers, plasterers, glaziers, plumbers, carvers and paviors – had probably been apprenticed for seven years. Once trained, it was their choice whether they worked permanently as journeymen or set up on their own. The London craftsman of the type who made himself a master builder, the capitalist of the building trade, was generally, as Sir John Summerson writes, 'a man of considerable skill and status – proud, conscientious, and expensive. He lived well and drank heartily. He was capable of writing a fairly good letter and could usually (if he were a mason, bricklayer or carpenter) make a plain "draught" of a small building.'

To operate on his own, this type of craftsman had to become a quasi-architect; but erecting small street houses had become easier now that these could be standard products, give or take a few floors, products which all the same made a receptive base for this or that style of front doorway or cornice. Practically the whole population of London lived in a terrace house standing joined to its neighbour on a narrow strip of ground. Those who built could copy other houses and study books. Books were the most important single factor in establishing Palladian taste throughout the building world, and several masons, carpenters and joiners were among subscribers for the first volume of Colen Campbell's *Vitruvius Britannicus* which dealt with English buildings of the seventeenth and early eighteenth centuries; this appeared in the same year, 1715, as an edition of Palladio brought out in instalments. Within ten years there began to flow from the presses a river of books compiled by craftsmen for craftsmen. The spirit in which they were written is indicated by the first paragraph of Batty Langley's *The City and Country Workman's Treasury of Design*, 1741 (Langley, a carpenter-surveyor, published twenty books from 1726):

> The great pleasure that builders and workmen of all kinds have of late years taken in the study of architecture; and the great advantages that have accrued to those, for whom they have been employed; by having their works executed in a much neater and more magnificent manner than was ever done in this Kingdom before; has been the real motive that induced me, to the compiling of this work, for their further improvement.

Many of the speculative houses, though neat and decorative, were not as robust as they appeared. Dan Cruikshank, in his fascinating book *London: the Art of Georgian Building*, offers evidence that architects of the eighteenth century were worried about speculative houses being technically ill-built for reasons of economy. He quotes Isaac Ware, writing in 1735:

> the nature of the tenures in London has introduced the art of building slightly [flimsily]. The ground landlord is to come into possession at the end of a short term and the builder, unless his grace ties him down to articles, does not choose to employ his money to his advantage. . . . It is for this reason we see houses built for 60, 70 or, the stoutest of the kind, for 99 years. They care they shall not stand longer than their time occasions, many to fall before it is expired; nay some have carried the art of building slightly so far, that their houses have fallen before they were tenanted.

These views were so generally held, writes Mr Cruikshank, that the Building Act of 1774 was largely concerned with measures to make houses stronger. In particular it was concerned with putting an end to the slipshod construction of party walls which had been a trial to Pepys in the seventeenth century.

To lay down hard and fast rules for builders, London houses

were categorized in detail and co-ordinated into the rates already referred to, from first rate down to fourth and fifth rate, and strict requirements were set out for each category. Thus, already, minimum standards were in force for little working-class houses, which might have been decent places to live in, had it been possible to legislate also against overcrowding.

With little now left to the builder's imagination, the Act led to a marked standardization of London streets and produced order and dignity in the later suburbs. We appreciate today what remains of this dignity, but it is understandable that the Victorians, contemplating larger areas of it than are now to be seen, talked about the terrible monotony of the typical London street.

London, of course, frankly expanded outwards and whole streets and squares could be built as one operation. It was different in the small market towns (very small indeed by modern standards) which no one at any time could have called monotonous: a prohibitive value was put on their surrounding fields, which supplied the inhabitants with easily carted-in food, and building operations had to be concentrated within existing boundaries – these operations largely consisting of additions and individually ordered re-frontings.

Colchester in Essex is one of the towns which had plenty of vacant sites within its walls, and a big middle-class expansion in the 1750s – most satisfactory for building workers – led to the creation of tight areas and groups of exemplary houses which were nevertheless slightly different from one another. Old rate books show that those who occupied them, and enjoyed the amenities of town life, were small industrialists, merchants, doctors, shopkeepers, builders, lawyers and lawyer-estate agents.

Such people gave the building trade its impetus to do good work. At Colchester it seems that there was an extra little incentive, that the more squalid the cottages and courts of the unfortunate, the more builders of the new houses sought to make every detail correct and in contrast with what was to be seen from the upper windows. The lower windows had robust internal shutters and the gardens protectively high brick walls.

4

BUILDERS AND LANDLORDS II

Before building undertakers could start on work in the towns, streets and building plots had to be planned and staked out on the ground. Each individual plot had to be leased or sold to them by a formal conveyance; if the conveyance was made after construction, there was an initial contract known as a building agreement to convey land once the work was finished.

The landlord in some cases prepared the sites, providing paved roads with sewers, and even credit for the builders: his profit came with the rise in the value of the land after it had become built up. From dukes to local tradespeople, numerous owners of land were attracted by the high potential rewards of conveying it in small pieces to builders. These in turn – and the bigger operators known as developers – made excellent profits in a housing boom at the end of the 1780s. However, in the depressed war years of the 1790s, which followed the boom, many landlords who had acquired land to sell, and many builders with the use of plots to build on, found their acquisitions left on their hands. In 1793, according to Mr Chalkin, three cotton merchants and another man took twenty acres of building land at Chorlton Row in Manchester, at a rent of £548 18s. 4d., but could dispose of hardly any of it; eventually, in 1808, three of the men assigned the whole estate to the fourth as a present, believing it to have no value. An oversupply of houses in fashionable Bath at this period brought down rents.

The class of housing to be erected on particular pieces of ground was considered in advance by the landlord, according to the kind of tenant he thought likely to come forward, and was generally achieved by clauses in the conveyance or building agreement. Where ordinary artisan houses seemed suitable, the restrictions imposed on the builder might be minimal. For example, the Duke of Newcastle did not even stipulate 'no offensive trades' when in 1807 he sold a Nottingham field divided into forty-two building plots. The duke had guessed that this absence of restrictions would suit the tenants he had in mind and, indeed, soon disposed of the plots at the then satisfactory rates of 6s. and 13s. a square yard. Elsewhere in Nottingham, by inserting strict clauses in his building agreements, he achieved 'select developments' containing houses of some pretension.

A usual kind of restriction on builders is exemplified by the rules laid down by the widow of a Nottingham banker, when she sold a site marked into numerous building plots: she required that every house should have an annual value of not less than £8 and forbade the formation, within four yards of a street, of 'a necessary house, dunghill, hogsty, cowhouse or noxious shed'.

At the top end of the scale, the houses of Bedford Square in London were intended to attract people with a high standard of living wanting a stylish, though not enormous, residence. The consequence, as Simon Jenkins has put it in *Landlords to London*, was the pseudo-palatial, terraced façade which was to remain the hallmark of London upper-middle-class architecture for the next century. Each house had its own imposing presence and was subtly related to all the others.

Robert Palmer, agent to the Duchess of Bedford, was largely responsible for Bedford Square. He had behind him the experience of haphazard development elsewhere, and he was prepared to go to great lengths to ensure that nothing would spoil the quality of the new neighbourhood: it in fact became a lawyers' district, being near the Inns of Court. The conditions which Palmer imposed on the builders went into minute details of proportion and materials; for example, the floors were to be of 'good yellow seasoned deals free from sap'. And no trade of any kind was to be carried on in the houses. Even the lesser streets, built to the north of Bedford Square, were to be forbidden ground to normal traders. A shopkeeper might not send his boy to make a delivery, though he himself would be admitted. Nothing was to lower the tone of the neighbourhood. Impressive visual results were possible on the great residential estates of London because there the plots were not leased singly, but in blocks, to builders required to group their houses carefully.

Landowners and builders might well be united in a desire to have lasting buildings of good appearance, but the landowners were in a safer position. As owners of the land they risked no more than a few years' ground rent. The developers, on whose shoulders rested the risk, were often with reason called

18 Small village-street Georgian house (Beccles, Suffolk). It has four rooms to a floor, but many houses with fronts like this had only two rooms to a floor.

adventurers; they could sacrifice everything. The Adam brothers, for instance, came near to ruin at the Adelphi, Charing Cross, when they failed to let the houses they had constructed there. The Duke of St Albans, from whom they had taken out a 99 year lease, lost nothing. Only a Government lottery, in which their houses were offered as prizes, managed to save them the day. The number of bankruptcies among Georgian builders was, as I have said, very high. There was none among the landowners, the freeholders.

One entirely successful builder-developer was Thomas Cubitt, who brought wealth and prestige to the Grosvenor Estate. His fascination with improved town planning led, in Pimlico, to a plethora of streets and squares crossed by a grid of diagonal streets; the houses were strictly residential.

Cubitt was the first builder of any kind to have his own fully equipped building firm in the modern manner; his company was complete with all the appropriate tradesmen, with foremen to match; it operated from workshops in Gray's Inn Road. Cubitt came into prominence when, early in the 1820s, the Duke of Bedford decided the time was ripe for further development north of Russell Square. A group of developers came forward to lease Woburn and Torrington Squares and the remainder fell to Cubitt, already well known for having a work force permanently on his books. He was the answer, as Mr Jenkins has pointed out, to every landowner's prayer; he had considerable knowledge of the house market and a steady nerve for risks. Watching his market as he went along, he steadily contracted for more and more of North Bloomsbury and brought all enterprises to a satisfactory conclusion.

As a general rule, houses were a very good investment in the eighteenth century. And plenty of people had money to invest. Savings were accumulating as a result of the expansion of home and foreign trade, more productive agriculture and the development of processing and manufacturing industry. In the main, only the aristocracy and members of the gentry invested in stocks and shares – and only those who lived within twenty or thirty miles of London. For the bulk of the people the normal outlet for money was a local investment, especially ownership of property.

Mr Chalkin has given as one example the wills of 158 Portsmouth residents, proved in the periods 1705–11 and 1721–24, which contain 49 references to houses owned by testators, the majority having more than one house. A similar pattern of house ownership is indicated by title deeds in Birmingham which show that between 1781 and 1820, 140 people bought the 470 new houses sold in that period, these representing all the more substantial townspeople. In the same way in Liverpool, between 1745 and 1800, the comparatively small number of 145 people were involved in the purchase of 269 houses, sold within twenty years of the lease of the site to a particular builder.

Anthemion and palmette

Flutes and paterae

Other paterae

Wheat-ear drop

Festoon of wheat-ear and pendants as on a ceiling or frieze

Plaque as on a chimney-piece

Guilloche pattern

Wave or scroll repeat

Fluted fan

   Urns and candlestick

19 Adam motifs were supplied ready-made for builders to stick on.

38

An investment of a rather similar kind, less often available, was the ownership of ground rents. Landowners sometimes sold the rents after houses had been built, these providing a regular income without the administrative duties of house ownership. One advantage, explained by an advertiser in the *Hull Advertiser*, was that, whether the premises were let or not, the proprietor of them was liable to pay the ground rent – of, say, 6 per cent – and when they were let, the owner of the ground rent could distrain for it.

5
THE FIRST TERRACE
HOUSES

The terrace house in its English form has long been taken for granted. Until a few years ago thousands were being pulled down every year in London alone, but now its numerous merits over the flat in a tall block (these blocks never seem to take up less space) have been so widely recognized that the rate of destruction has been much reduced. In 1976 the Greater London Council promised to renew dwellings only with terrace housing. Although the earliest terrace houses have a Georgian air, they first made their appearance well before the start of the Georgian period.

Small, single-fronted houses were in fact devised for London in almost their final form during the reign of Charles II. Two rooms deep, as regular as the bricks composing them, they seemed very fresh at that time and agreeably foreign, like a stage set, among what remained after the Great Fire of gabled and jettied-out buildings in wood. The verticality of these houses (each with a

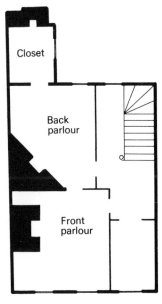

20   Plan of late seventeenth-to-early-eighteenth-century terrace house.

scrap of walled garden) was being willingly accepted at a period when in most continental cities people were learning to live horizontally in flats. Already Georgian-looking, they set a drill for London streets which has now been approved of for three centuries.

Nicholas Barbon, Member of Parliament and speculative builder, put up rows of such houses in the 1670s and was described by Roger North, his lawyer contemporary, as 'the inventor of this new method of casting ground into streets and small houses . . . each with as little front as possible'. Roger North (*Autobiography* quoted by Sir John Summerson in *Georgian London*) was right about use of the ground if not about Barbon inventing it, for brick had become obligatory after the panic of the Fire and yellowish earth to feed the brick moulds was taken from the nearest convenient point. Digging for cellars and cesspools often yielded loads of material suitable for adequate red bricks (insistence on yellow ones came much later), and building went ahead with burning clamps standing about, troubling workmen on nearby scaffolding with their fumes.

Bricks had a welcome regularity as components for the new, English-classical, terrace houses. It was Palladian architecture, introduced by Inigo Jones (see the Italian dress of Lindsey House in Lincoln's Inn Fields, *c.*1630), which had shown the way to profitable standardization and to an appreciation of symmetry. Barbon's little houses hardly varied; the ornament inside, the panels and the twisted stair balusters were mass produced and did not vary at all. Examples of the brand can be seen in Bedford Row (Nos 36, 42 and 43) and in Great Ormond Street (Nos 55 and 57).

Massive brickwork was stipulated in the post-Fire building regulations. Even houses of 'the first and least sort' (two storeys besides cellar and attic) were required, up to first floor level, to have 'front and back walls of a thickness of the length of two bricks'. Where there was one more storey these walls had to be two and a half bricks thick, just under two feet. The obligation to handle so many bricks during a building boom brought a great shortage of skilled bricklayers, and for the first time London men

21 A contemporary's depiction of the Great Fire of London done from the south bank of the Thames; it shows the Tower and Whitehall unscathed on either side of billowing flames and smoke. A German copperplate engraving of 1670.

were allowed by Act of Parliament to lay bricks without being members of the Guild.

Sir Christopher Wren, architect of Chelsea Hospital, seemed able to get good men to achieve his delightful effects in rubbed brick with stone dressings, but lesser men building ordinary streets late in the seventeenth century had to take a proportion of indifferent bricklayers. Joseph Moxon is critical of their work in the brickwork section of his *Mechanick Exercises*, 1678, in particular of the 'ill custom of some bricklayers to carry up a whole storey of party walls before they work up the fronts that should be bonded with them'. This, he said, occasioned cracks.

Failures often led to a quick re-building. Delayed trouble, not foreseen by Moxon, has been caused by getting the neatest workman to run up an outer skin of smart brickwork against an inner, rougher section of wall. There was no keying in of any kind and the heavier inside part, supporting joists, tended to sink further than the outside part. Bulges mar the fronts of house after house in Great Ormond Street; they have been contained, not more, by recent insertion of tie rods and plates. When repair work exposes all, it is seen that the headers of the Flemish bond pattern are half bricks or conveniently used-up bats. Many fronts were rebuilt within about fifty years because of surface crumbling of soft bricks. Again fake Flemish bond was presented, but eighteenth-century bricklayers did make an effort every eight courses or so to attach the outer skin to its backing. (Bastard bonds are sometimes pleasantly used now to avoid the dullness of continuous stretchers in the modern, metal-tied cavity wall.)

Delayed trouble of a more serious kind, pointed at today as grounds for demolition, is the result of following the advice of Moxon himself to lay wooden beams in the footings and to insert 'bond timbers' at various heights in the walls for strengthening. As the wood shrinks, or crumbles from dry rot, so the walls get weaker than they would have been without it, and so uneven settling occurs: in upper storeys I have noticed slips of up to seven inches, but even so there may be no actual cracks because the old lime mortar 'gives', allowing bricks to readjust their positions instead of breaking.

22   Italian Renaissance design for a small street house in Rome by
Giulio Romano, mid sixteenth century.

23   Late eighteenth-century continuous row of London terrace houses.

Apart from slipping, none of the early terrace houses in London looks quite as it did when built. Casement window frames with transom bars were changed early in the eighteenth century for the ingenious sash type from Holland, a type which became so widely valued that at least one labourer refused to live in a new cottage with casement windows, saying they were tokens of inferior social status – C. F. Innocent, *The Development of English Building Construction*, 1916. Changes in the look of the fabric were brought about by successive Acts designed to reduce the danger of fire. A London Act of 1707 banished visible tiled roofs and wooden eaves cornices behind a classical brick parapet. From 1708 the walls of new houses – and in time those of many older ones – took on a more solid air through conforming with a regulation that a four-inch reveal of brickwork should protect door and window frames. These had previously been set flush with the face of walls.

To read Henry Fielding on the lack of policing at this time and on houses being maliciously set alight from outside, is to realize that the attempts to banish external and accessible wooden features was inspired not only by fear of fires started accidentally. The fire hazard caused protective window shutters to be fitted inside most houses, and not outside as on the Continent. These shutters for downstairs rooms, either neatly folding or moveable up or down on the sash window principle, needed to be strong as well as attractively joinered. Mobs expressed their feelings from time to time. Want at this time drove many to try breaking and entering, to what the *Kentish Gazette* in 1768 called 'violent invasions of property'.

The beauty of the brick mansions of Queen Anne's reign spread downwards and showed itself in ordinary terrace housing. In London the unnecessary massiveness of walls for small houses was reduced, by permission, to a maximum thickness of a brick and a half (thirteen inches), and builders were asked to take more trouble over bonding the bricks together.

Brickyards became more efficient. They were still set up as near as possible to work in progress, but in addition there were semi-permanent yards in the outer suburbs. Georgian bricks came to range in quality from hard 'stocks' for outer walls to ashy place bricks for unseen party walls (timber-framed room partitions long continued usual). Windsor and Kentish rubbers, crimson bricks that could be easily rubbed or sawn to shape, arrived in London by barge for the forming of window arches for almost every kind of house.

In the 1730s experiment with Palladianism became a major function for the amateur architects, who did much to spread new ideas (professional architects emerged later in the century); their

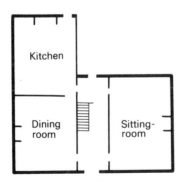

24　Plan of early Victorian L-shaped terrace house with kitchen in rear wing: the double front gives a well-to-do appearance.

ideal façade presented a pilastered symmetry raised on a robust-looking lower floor representing the Roman podium, and hints of this style even showed themselves in the fronts of minor terrace houses. The bricklayers, as they worked on these (each itself shaped rather like a brick on end) took to new ways with facing bricks to enhance, with suggestions of classical motifs, England's best housing invention, the narrow Georgian terrace house. Flats involve less climbing, but who has ever had the satisfaction of repainting the outside of a flat or been able to keep rabbits in a communal hall or recreation area?

6

LIVING IN
LONDON

Among good examples of the earliest eighteenth-century terrace houses in London are the ten of Queen Anne brick in Cheyne Row, Chelsea. They are solidly built houses, all designed to the same plan, with, on each floor, two well-proportioned panelled rooms and the then-usual small closet opening out of the back room. Inevitably the passing years have brought changes. Most of the houses have had attic rooms added, one was given a Victorian portico and two of them Victorian balconies.

A particular house known to me, No. 24 (formerly No. 5), was the home for much of his life of Thomas Carlyle. Since he and his wife Jane were voluminous letter writers, a vivid record remains of what a modest-sized house in Chelsea was like at the close of the Georgian period, and of conditions of life there. Thea Holme, making use of the correspondence, has written of the house in her books *Jane Welsh Carlyle* and *Chelsea*.

Carlyle himself chose it and sent favourable descriptions to his wife of the panelled rooms, the carved staircase with its spirally-turned balusters, the numerous cupboards and closets. Jane suspected the panelling of harbouring bugs (on that ground people had for years been tearing panelling from their rooms in favour of plaster or wallpaper), but it proved to be in good order and is still there today.

The already-famous historian and his wife set up residence with one maid. Previously the only occupant to make a mark on the house was John Tarbit Knowles, who had scratched on a back window pane that on 7 March 1794, he had 'cleaned all the windows and painted part in the 18 years of his age'. The Carlyles' maid had her bed in the front kitchen and kept her clothes in the wash-house. Little attention was given in those days to where servants slept, and as late as the 1880s Oscar Wilde's manservant slept in an alcove between the second and third floors of No. 16, Tite Street, Chelsea. Between the second and third floors at No. 24, Cheyne Row, the Carlyles found a mysterious cupboard with a window. Mrs Holme, who with her husband Stanford was a recent occupant of the house, believes this cupboard to have been a place for a page boy to sleep; and she has recorded the finding of two partitioned recesses with

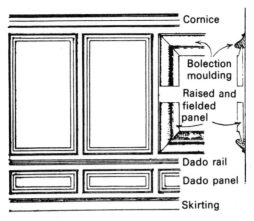

25 Late seventeenth- and early eighteenth-century wall panelling. This, in the form popularized by Wren, was a matter of rules. About two feet nine inches from the floor ran a three-inch dado rail. Above this were tall panels, their width commensurate with the size of the room; and below, between dado rail and skirting, squat panels squared up with those above. Each panel was framed in a bolection (projecting) moulding and the fielded panel raised from the line of the wall.

primitive wooden ventilators, evidently maids' bedrooms, in the basement kitchen of another house in Cheyne Row.

Constant noise was a fact of life in this part of Chelsea. Leigh Hunt, the essayist who was living there when the Carlyles arrived, claimed to have enjoyed the trade cries of people selling such things as cowslips and primroses and buns. 'There was an old seller of fish in particular whose cry of "Shrimps as large as prawns!" was such a regular, long-drawn and truly pleasing melody, that in spite of the hoarse and, I'm afraid, drunken voice, I used to wish for it of an evening, and hail it when it came.'

The street noises of the suburb had a different reception from the Carlyles, who would doubtless have installed double or treble glazing had it been available. They had come from a remote farmhouse in Scotland where the silence was so intense that sheep could be heard cropping the grass. In Chelsea, Jane wrote to her cousin, 'there is an everlasting sound of men, women, children, omnibuses, carriages ... the very air seems to vibrate with

26 Regency street vendors in London. Leigh Hunt said he enjoyed the melody of the trade cries floating into his rooms.

activity.' At first she was able to remark cheerfully that the 'stirring life' was more to her mind than silence and had 'a beneficial effect on my bowels', but as time went by both Carlyles found the noise at times insupportable. As well as the hawkers' cries, there were carts and hand-barrows of all kinds rattling over the cobble stones, accompanied by shouts from drivers to their animals. Carlyle almost lost his temper when one day a Punch and Judy show joined in the din. 'An accursed Punch is shrieking under my windows. The curtains keep out squalid sights; but how exclude distractive sounds?'

He spent the next thirty years, Mrs Holme has written, trying to find the answer, years during which Jane had often to write diplomatic letters to keepers of cocks, parrots and macaws, parents of music-practising young ladies and owners of barking dogs, begging, bribing, cajoling, even offering her services as instructress to a backward child, to obtain a few hours' silence for her author husband. The noises – or their power to distract him – changed with the years. After a so-called silent room had been arranged at the top of the house, the crowing of cocks in the next-door garden passed unremarked, but his attentions, Jane said, were now 'morbidly devoted to Railway Whistles'.

Other parts of London had noises more brutal in character than those of Chelsea. A lot of people almost lived in the streets, their homes being only sleeping dens (the slums of Drury Lane, St Giles, Southwark, and Clerkenwell grew worse as the Georgian period advanced), and the cries of sweeps, coalmen, milkmaids, newsmen, knife-grinders – each with his particular call – were accompanied by the clatter of well-laden, iron-rimmed wheels and the curses of chair men and porters forcing a passage along narrow streets. Everyone, it seems, bawled and was ready in a moment to put down a load, or jump from a coach, to finish an argument with punches.

Crime was everywhere, as in all great cities, and pickpockets were busy wherever people gathered. No regular police force existed, only the parish constables, and the watch who patrolled at night, calling out the time; they did little to protect the ordinary citizens. In addition to regular criminals, there were gangs of well-born young men who enjoyed roaming the streets tying up door knockers and causing embarrasment. Harmless

27 Regency knife grinder. Handbarrows of all kinds rattled over the cobble stones.

people could be set upon without reason, their coach or sedan chair overturned, their clothes smeared. One gang was known as the Mohocks. Dean Swift once wrote of having come 'home in a chair for fear of the Mohocks', seemingly unaware that the mere sight of a sedan chair at night could invite attack.

The magistrates, the parish constables and the often elderly watchmen could not begin to control London's crime. When damage-causing riots occurred, and these were always likely on any excuse, the soldiers were called in and there might be loss of life: the citizens detested soldiers and made their mere appearance an excuse for greater violence.

Rewards were offered for the capture of thieves, who found that by tempting boys into crime they could receive the rewards themselves for informing on them. Jonathan Wild made money from 'thief taking'; he also arranged robberies, received the goods and sold them back to their owners. He was in due course executed. The Fielding brothers, who were paid magistrates at Bow Street, made matters a little better by forming a body of reliable men to arrest footpads and track robbers; these men wore red waistcoats and were known as both Robin Redbreasts and Bow Street Runners. In 1783 the Treasury paid for a police horse patrol to operate in the roads around London. This reduced highway robbery so soon that the patrol was disbanded, and naturally the robbers returned. The usefulness of a regular police force had, however, been demonstrated.

The threat of death, in force for over a hundred offences in the eighteenth century, may have actually increased crime because, where a thief could be hanged for taking a watch, he might decide to kill its owner to avoid later being recognized. And when the theft of any article worth more than 5s. could be punished by death, those robbed would often reduce the value of a stolen article to spare a life, possibly that of a starving child.

In all these circumstances, the provision of a sense of safety was a big consideration in house construction: hence the stout front door, the efficient internal shutters, the spiked railings calculated to prevent entry – accidental or purposeful – to basement areas. A person's trim classical house, civilized within, provided a

haven from the roar of London. 'Shut up in our apartments,'
wrote Louis Simond, 'we listen to its waves, breaking around us
in measured time.'

Louis Simond, an American brought up in France, was a most
perceptive foreign visitor and writer. It fascinated him to
consider the standard Georgian houses of London, the result of a
hundred years of Georgian building, and he wrote of them in
1810 in his *Journal of a Tour* (as it has since been called), a work he
translated for French readers. 'It may be a matter of curiosity in
France', he wrote, 'to know how the people of London are
lodged.'

Each family occupies a whole house, unless very poor. There
are advantages and disadvantages attending this custom.
Among the first, the being more independent of the noise,
the dirt, the contagious disorders, or the danger of your
neighbour's fires, and having a more complete home. On
the other hand, an apartment all on one floor, even of a few
rooms only [as was usual in Paris] looks better and is more
convenient. These narrow houses, three or four stories high –
one for eating, one for sleeping, a third for company, a
fourth under ground for the kitchen, a fifth perhaps at the
top for servants – and the agility, the ease, the quickness
with which the individuals of the family run up and down,
and perch on the different stories – give the idea of a cage
with its sticks and birds.

The plan of these houses is very simple, two rooms on
each storey; one in the front with two or three windows
looking on to the street, the other on a yard behind, often
very small; the stairs generally taken out of the breadth of
the back room. The ground-floor is usually elevated a few
feet above the level of the street, and separated from it by an
area, a sort of ditch, a few feet wide. . . . A bridge of stone or
brick leads to the door of the house. The front of these
houses is about twenty or twenty-five feet wide; they
certainly have a rather paltry appearance – but you cannot
pass the threshold without being struck with the look of

28 Orderly wigs, even sometimes for children, were part of a middle class striving for order in classical houses. Mid-eighteenth-century print.

order and neatness of the interior. Instead of the abominable filth of the common entrance and common stairs of a French house, here you step from the very street on a neat floor cloth or carpet, the walls painted or papered, a lamp in its glass bell hanging from the ceiling, and every apartment in the same style – all is neat, compact and independent, or, as it is best expressed here, snug and comfortable.

Primitive ways of getting water for domestic use did not seem odd to Simond, for these were no better in Paris. Until the beginning of the nineteenth century, the water for a few public standcocks in the streets, and for houses with a tap, came through underground wooden pipes, which might be logs with a hole driven through them. From these, there were small lead pipes branching out to houses; but in general it was only houses on the great London estates which were so connected – they received a trickle of water for a few hours on certain days.

Those who managed these residential estates imposed all kinds of restrictions on their tenants, for their own good, and to keep their surroundings exclusive, as in the case of Bedford Square referred to. For people with the money to live in them, life was peaceful. Simond wrote of a ramble with a friend through 'several large squares, planted in the middle with large trees and shrubs, over a smooth lawn, interspersed with gravel walks; the whole enclosed by an iron railing, which protects these gardens against the populace, but does not intercept the view. The inhabitants of the neighbourhood, who contribute to the expense, have each a key.' In such parts of London, Simond had 'heard no cries in the streets, seen few beggars, nor obstructions or stoppages of carriages, each taking to the left.'

7

BUILDING
MATERIALS AND
ECONOMY

Brick had overtaken wood as the predominant building material by the 1780s and curiously smelly brickyards were common on the outskirts of many towns. The smell, only partly sulphurous, was unlike any brickmaking smell today, and Simond cannot have been alone in not understanding why the air in the brickyard districts around London was 'poisoned by the emanations from brick kilns, exactly like carrion, to such a degree as to excite nausea'.

The explanation is that the brickmakers were relying for their process on tons of partially rotted household garbage carted away from town centres. The valuable ingredient in this unpleasant material was the remains of coal fires. The cinders and scraps of coal were spread in layers through the clamps of raw bricks to fire them, and the ash was mixed with the actual brickmaking clay to help the bricks to go white hot under firing – and also, by reducing the plasticity of clay, to prevent them from cracking.

The use of all this rubbish was most effective in more than keeping down the price of bricks: the famous yellow stock bricks of London owe much of their durability to an admixture of domestic coal ash. Even today there are brick firms which put a lot of ash into their mixture, but modern ways of heating houses has so much reduced the supply of fuel from dustbins that they must buy the sludge that arises at coal washeries – a material that has no putrid additives.

It has always been a fact of building practice that various kinds of rubbish and unpromising matter can be put to good use. Building houses with earth straight from the ground has been described already: over half the world's dwellings are mud houses and scores have been built in England in the twentieth century. Breeze blocks make no secret of what they are made of and many modern walling units are demonstrably composed of waste paper.

However, taking rubbish to build with was overdone in the rising industrial towns of the late eighteenth and nineteenth centuries, and concern was expressed about mortar being made with road sweepings, dirty sand and only a pretence of lime.

Although the bedding between bricks need not be as hard as the bricks themselves – indeed some tolerance to allow for settlement is desirable – there are limits beyond which the best laid brickwork will not stay in position. Mortar dropping out as dust has caused, sooner or later, the disintegration of numerous otherwise satisfactory houses.

Restrictions caused by the drawn-out Napoleonic wars almost doubled building costs between 1790 and 1810, and as housing densities in manufacturing towns increased because of a rise in population and higher prices for land, so did skimping on building materials. Most readers will have noticed the painful thinness of damp-spotted bedroom walls in run-of-the-mill Regency houses.

Just after the turn of the century Simond described the rows of houses he saw being built, new ones rising daily, as he travelled north out of London. 'As if to destroy the little solidity of which such thin walls are capable, they generally place window above a pier below, and a pier above the window below. ... I am informed that it is made an express condition in the leases of these shades of houses that there shall be no dances given in them.' In certain new terrace houses in Nottingham to hold a dance in upper rooms was out of the question, to judge by a contemporary's report that feeble joists were set so far apart that floors laid on them sank to the tread.

It may happen today that repairs to floors of houses dating from the early part of the nineteenth century reveal joists consisting of odd lengths of timber, some mere branches, some set diagonally.

This economical use of timber in the structure of floors was facilitated by the now-established practice of ceiling below with laths and plasters. Covering up in this way was first resorted to because joists of mere imported softwood were not deemed worthy of exposure; but soon even the best construction with local hardwood was also hidden by a ceiling; the oak-beamed look which had for so long characterized the English parlour was no longer in fashion.

Lower standards of house carpentry and bricklaying were also

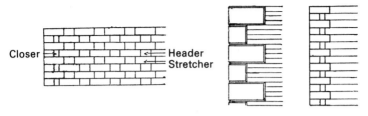

29 Bricklaying. Left: Flemish bond. Middle: dressed stone quoins, sometimes simulated with plaster or wood. Right: special quoin bricks laid with very fine joints.

conveniently hidden by smooth expanses of stucco (imitating stone and tinted cream or faun) for which architects had created a nationwide taste. Today the stucco is often found to mask poorly laid, salmon-pink bricks too soft and porous to have survived uncovered.

Stucco made possible the proverbial splendour of the fairy-tale terraces by John Nash at Regent's Park in London: but these were speculative buildings, and behind the elegant shapes and surfaces was jerry building. When some of the seeming palaces came to be restored in the mid-twentieth century, complete reconstruction inside was necessary and hollow portico columns of underburnt brick needed much strengthening. Nash of course produced other buildings that were perfectly solid (Buckingham Palace in its present form was his), yet such were the economic conditions of his time that his speculative buildings have given him a certain reputation for shoddy work.

In some of the rising manufacturing towns, bricks were used sparingly because of the tax that was put on them in 1784 to cover the expenses of war with America, but builders were also influenced in some districts by the expense of transporting them – suitable brickearth to make them with was not always available nearby. In the south-east there was increased wood-framing in deal, either throughout a house or above first floor level. Tiles, slates or overlapping boards hung on such framing were weatherproof and an acceptable alternative to brick in appearance.

30   Fires lit beside thin, propped walls to encourage poor-quality mortar to set.

The softwood was imported from both Scandinavia and North America and, although comparatively a cheap building material, it rose in price from the late 1790s much faster than the rents or prices that could be achieved for houses. To skimp and to squeeze profit margins were necessary for builders if they were to make a living. Telling quotes from this period appear in Chalkin. In 1796 the Foundling Hospital Estate of London expressed the fear that the walls of buildings being erected for them had 'insufficient bond timbers to hold them together and therefore the walls would be apt in settling to give way and separate'. A London surveyor wrote in 1807: 'If I had pressed the builders to the extent of the power I possessed under their contracts, most of them would have failed.'

In view of their difficulties, builders were amazingly active; unfortunately, by building on and on to gain a living they caused in some places an over-supply and a consequent reduction in house prices. In 1795 a speculative builder in Birmingham was accepting ground rent only for his new houses in The Crescent.

Economies in the construction of ordinary houses were often accompanied by a charming precision in the finish of their fronts. The brickwork of late eighteenth-century small houses and cottages – before stucco covered all – often presents, for example,

Flemish bond beautifully executed with thin joints, and header bricks of a darker colour arranged in a pattern. But here, too, an economical trick was played. The headers were nearly always just half bricks, or ends, instead of bricks thrusting through the wall to strengthen it; again and again present-day repair operations reveal that the outer skin of a house front is not tied to the rest of the wall.

8

THE FARMHOUSE

The farmhouses seem as though just built. . . . The pleasing impression produced by invariable neatness and order, increases the admiration of the stranger, who will often mistake the dwelling of a plain farmer, for the residence of an independent gentleman. (Goede, *The Stranger in England*, an impression of the Dover road in 1802.)

The eighteenth century became a great time for farmhouse building in the productive lowlands of England. As one Enclosure Act followed another during the reign of George III, small yeoman farmers and independent peasants were bought out to make room for large, compact farm holdings to be cultivated by lucky tenant farmers. For these people, modern farmhouses were built out on the new holdings. Contemporaries have said that they were like little kings with their acres of hedged fields; that they were absorbed by their occupations, profusely hospitable at times, inclined to be arrogant and gratuitously insulting. If the image of the Georgian farmer changed for the worse, a part of the cause seems to have been the pattern of life suggested to him by his new house.

The pre-Georgian farmhouse, often in a village street, was of the irregular, long-house type with a string of large rooms and any number of outbuildings for washing, baking, brewing, dairy work and storage. A chimney stack of several flues rose asymmetrically from the house; the front door opened on to a tiny porch terminated by the base of this stack, behind which clung a circular stair leading to dormitories; on one side was the great kitchen living room with another room beyond it and, on the other side, a parlour, which was probably used as a bedroom.

This most unmonumental design did not suit Renaissance practice and early in the eighteenth century farmhouses began to conform to the classical pattern, with a balanced, five-windowed front, four rooms to a floor – and only a few separate sheds for household use. Like any other small Georgian houses, they had a chimney, or pair of chimneys, at each side to allow room for an entrance hall and a fine staircase in the middle. Many of the occupants of the new farmhouses were glad to acknowledge

31 Scene of gluttony amidst an elegant dumbwaiter (left) and visually perfect glass and crockery. Rowlandson, c. 1800.

32 Typical eighteenth-century farmhouse as it is likely to look today.

classicism by sporting a superficial central pediment at roof level. Porticos, too, appeared, though most farmers shied away from them, unlike the parsons who wished, by having such a feature, to show that they belonged to the gentry.

These new farmhouses helped to erode old traditions. Losing the irregular vernacular plan, and with it a commodious all-purpose kitchen, signified more than submission to the over-whelming Renaissance fashion; it signified, as M. W. Barley has written in *The English Farmhouse and Cottage*, the disappearance of a way of life based on comradeship and its replacement by one of farmers and labourers, employers and employees.

In the Lake District and other highland regions the old way of life long persisted. The farmer took his seat at night on the chimney settle with, nearby, his wife at her worktable and his daughters darning and trimming their hats. On the other side of the hearth, with their shoes off, sat the men of the farm. The farmer enjoyed talking over his work and plans with the men, discussing when to sow or reap, arranging what to do the next day. In Norfolk, on the other hand, the well-to-do farmer and his wife, newly housed, no longer sat with the farmworkers in the evening; there was no space for everyone in small square houses with small square rooms, and workers could no longer be treated as members of the family rather than employees.

The living conditions of unmarried farm servants unable to sleep in the farmhouse represents as bad a blot on eighteenth-century rural life as the cottages of married servants. According to J. C. Loudon, writing in the Regency period, the sleeping quarters of those men still fed by the farmer were 'in most parts of Britain generally such as to merit extreme reprobation ... frequently in lofts over stable or cow-houses, without light or sufficient space for air; subject to the deleterious exhalations arising from horse or cow dung; sometimes under a roof insufficient to exclude the wind and the rain'. The fortunate workers were those who could move into the abandoned village-street farmhouses, now subdivided to provide cottages.

The new manners of certain farmers, inspired by a stylish little house, became especially noticeable in eastern England and in the Home Counties and were remarked on by visitors from abroad. The eye of Jean Bernard Le Blanc was caught by the well-to-do farmers and he wrote in *Letters on the English and French Nations*, 1747, of luxury reigning as much in the countryside of England as in the cities of France.

> The English farmer is rich and enjoys all the conveniences of life in abundance. . . . One perceives by the houses of the English farmers that they are in easy circumstances enough to have a taste for neatness, and that they have likewise time to satisfy it. I have found them everywhere well clothed. They never go out without a riding coat. Their wives and daughters not only dress, but adorn themselves. . . . 'Tis a pity this plenty which the English farmer enjoys should make him so proud and insolent. He does not only dispute the road with those whom the order of society has made his superiors, but sometimes jostles and insults them for his pleasure.

Pehr Kalm, a Swede visiting England in 1748, reported seeing

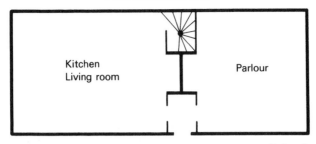

33 Asymmetrical plan of the seventeenth-century small farmhouse.

bands of farm servants at work in the fields with perukes on their heads, a circumstance which may or may not indicate affectation on the part of their employers.

In fact, farmers had often done much to be proud of. Daniel Defoe in his *Tour* of 1724–7 described an area to the west of London as 'plain and pleasant country, with a rich fertile soil, cultivated and enclosed to the utmost perfection of husbandry. . . . It is impossible to view these countries from any rising ground and not be ravished with the delightful prospect.'

The Enclosure Acts, which grew fast in number throughout the eighteenth century, both improved the look of the country and encouraged, as was their main intention, much more profitable agriculture: in the first ten years of the century one Enclosure Act only was passed, but in the period 1750–60, 156 were passed and in the period 1790–1800, 506. J. H. Plumb, author of *England in the Eighteenth Century*, cited evidence for increased profitability in rising figures for the average weight of cattle sold at Smithfield: a like number of oxen and sheep weighing 370 and 38 pounds in 1710 weighed at the end of the century respectively 800 and 80 pounds.

The prosperous farmer's new way of presenting himself often proved to be no more than a veneer over tenacious habits. The front path to his trim central entrance might be flanked by trees, yet no more used than his front parlours, everyone taking as a matter of course a muddy route to the door of the kitchen. Muddy surroundings with stagnant pools were said by William Howitt in *Rural Life in England* to be 'one of the greatest drawbacks to the pleasantness of the farmers' abodes'. In winter, he reported, the yards had a six-inch depth of mire – through which, however, the farmers and their men strode 'as unconcernedly as if on a Turkey carpet'. There was 'scarcely a farmhouse but has one of those drain pools into which the liquid refuse of the yard runs and into which dead dogs and cats find their way as a matter of course.'

It appears that after a honeymoon period with his villa residence, the farmer and his wife commonly began acting as their parents had, cluttering up their small rooms, including places where the family slept, with such produce as green fruit, bacon and new-made cheese. Charles Waistell, writing for an encyclopaedia of agricultural buildings at the end of the Georgian period, listed some surprising articles kept in the new-style farmhouses, articles which in his view contaminated the air and from which 'farmers and their families not infrequently suffer in their healths, without being, perhaps, at all aware of their pernicious effects'. These things, 'rendering the air of rooms unwholesome', included oil, oil colours, impure wool, sweaty saddles, tallow, fat, raw and dressed meat, foul linen, saffron and hops: the last two items had sometimes proved fatal. Even the most classical-looking Georgian farmhouse sometimes had low, ill-ventilated garrets, and dark closets used for storing what Waistell called the coarser articles and 'in these, very often, were lodged the female servants of the farmer'.

The last three decades of the eighteenth century saw brief bursts of spectacular cottage-building for rural labourers – cottages of brick, stone or of timber framework finished with plaster or weatherboards, though the number achieved was puny beside the need. These good cottages, which dot parts of the countryside today, were the exceptions, the work of estate-owners who were rich or benevolent, or who wished to seem so for reasons of prestige. All the rest have gone. Indeed, apart from specimens in villages, there are few true cottages in Britain earlier than mid-Georgian; the small stone or half-timber buildings we talk of as Tudor or Jacobean cottages were in their day the substantial houses of such people as yeoman farmers. All the evidence makes it fair to say that during the whole of the

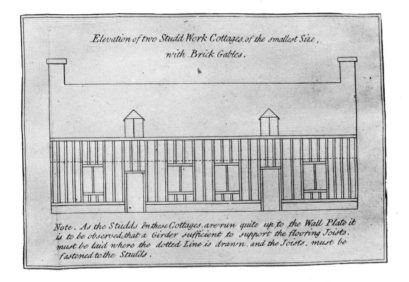

Elevation of two Studd Work Cottages, of the smallest Size,
with Brick Gables.

Note. As the Studds in these Cottages, are run quite up to the Wall Plate it
is to be observed, that a Girder sufficient to support the flooring Joists,
must be laid where the dotted Line is drawn, and the Joists, must be
fastened to the Studds.

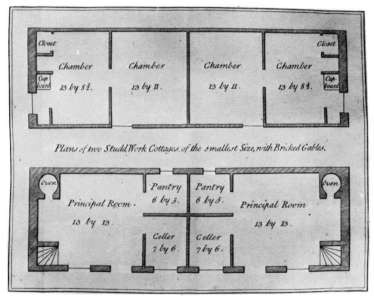

Plans of two Studd Work Cottages, of the smallest Size, with Bricked Gables.

34 Model semi-detached cottages. From Nathaniel Kent, *Hints to Gentlemen of Landed Property*, 1775.

Georgian period the majority of married farm workers lived in hovels, often self-built, that were far from Georgian in appearance. The accommodation commonly amounted to one room, though some of the hovels had a lean-to shed. In certain districts the chimneys were still being made of poles daubed with clay. Furze was believed to be a good fuel and was widely collected from the commons.

The first pattern book devoted entirely to workers' cottages was John Wood's *Series of Plans for Cottages or Habitations of the Labourer*. Before producing it, John Wood (he was the designer of the Royal Crescent and other terraces in Bath) went to look at existing cottages near Bath, subsequently making strictures that were by no means unusual at this period, or later. 'The greater part of those that fell within my observation', he wrote, 'I found to be shattered, dirty, inconvenient, miserable hovels, scarcely affording a shelter for the beasts of the forest, much less were they proper habitations for the human species.' He noted that often a man and his wife and some half-dozen children had to crowd together at night in the same bed. Wood's simple cottages, some having two rooms only, were markedly classical. He insisted on regularity, which in his view was beauty, and would add blind windows and doors to give an axial and symmetrical façade without imposing on the convenience of the plan. The cottages were in truth convenient and practical in their simple way. Wood made the point, which is as valid as ever now, that if cottages are built in pairs 'the inhabitants may be of assistance to each other in case of sickness or any other accident'. An idea still lingered in the country that the south wind brought the plague, and main windows therefore faced north. But Wood said: 'Let the window of the main room receive its light from the East or the South; then it will be always warm and cheerful . . . so like the feelings of men in an higher sphere are those of the poor cottager, that if his habitation be warm cheerful and comfortable, he will return to it with gladness, and abide in it with pleasure.'

Semi-detached cottages came to be built in large numbers by a minority of land owners wishing to provide improved housing for their workers; they were economical to build, and also economical to heat where one central chimney stack warmed both sides. The type was not a new invention, however: semi-detached cottages were built by Lord Orford at Chippenham in Cambridgeshire in the last years of the seventeenth century. An interesting point about the farm worker's semi is that it is a rare example of a worker's dwelling which has risen in the social scale.

Meanwhile, the classical Georgian farmhouses, which when first built had looked incongruous amid the farmery, became increasingly knocked about; a century and a half after their erection, many contained no item of upholstered furniture. It may be that today farming and non-farming occupants are, for the first time in the history of these houses, treating them in the manner called for by their neat and elegant design.

In America it was rare in the first half of the nineteenth century to see a satisfactory farmhouse, according to A. J. Downing in his influential book *The Architecture of Country Houses*. Yet 80 per cent of the population lived in them. Downing was at pains to point out that good forms, having 'an air of rustic plainness', need not cause additional cost. His view, which theoretically met critics of England's villa farmhouses, was this:

Our farmers are by no means all contented with a comfortable shelter for their heads. On the contrary, we see numberless attempts to give something of beauty to their homes. The designs continually published by agricultural journals, most of which emanate from the agricultural class, show the continual aiming after something better, which characterizes every class in this country. Some of these designs are appropriate and tasteful. But a large number of the better and more substantial farmhouses . . . are decidedly failures, considered either in a tasteful or architectural point of view. They are often failures not because there are no evidences of comfort or beauty in their exteriors or interiors; but because they are not truthful; because they do not express the life and character of the farmer; because they neglect their own true and legitimate sources of interest, and aim to attain beauty by imitating or

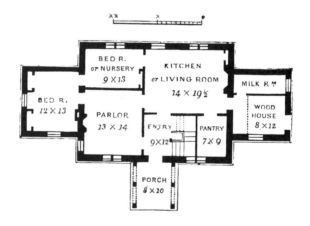

35 A North American farmhouse of the first half of the nineteenth century 'with the merit of expressing the subject, of looking like a farmhouse'. From A. J. Downing, *The Architecture of Country Houses*.

borrowing the style of decorations of the ornamental cottage or villa.

Downing provided pictures and plans of farmhouses in the Gothic, Swiss, Old English, Southern States, villa and other styles. One which is simply called 'symmetrical stone farmhouse' (see page 74) lives up to his list of requirements and has the merit, as he says, of 'expressing the subject, of looking like a farmhouse'.

Downing writes further that the building is intended to accommodate

the family of a farmer in comfortable circumstances – a family above want, independent through its own labour, but with little or no superfluous means. Such a family will prize convenience, snugness and comfort more than display; and we have endeavoured to meet its wishes by making the living-room or kitchen the best and largest room in the house – with a good pantry, a wood-house, a milk-room, and a bedroom or nursery, all communicating with it – so that as few steps as possible need be taken to perform the household labours. The parlour is placed in an appropriate and accessible position – communicating with the front entry – and opening into a bedroom, which . . . could always be reached from the kitchen without going through the parlour, by passing through the nursery or children's bedroom.

Plenty of modern farmhouses in use in Britain today have a similar appearance and plan: it is a pre-Georgian plan. A tenant farmer known to me who lives in a house similar to the one illustrated, so much prizes the snugness and comfort that he declined to move into a larger and more imposing farmhouse when it was offered to him by the landowner.

75

9

THE PARSONAGE

Most parsonages in the Georgian period were thatched cottages with earth floors. They were poor and simple like the typical occupant, though improvements occurred here and there as a result of the setting-up in 1704 of Queen Anne's Bounty. Even in William Halfpenny's book of model designs for parsonages, published in 1753, only utility buildings are put forward: they have the fashionable balanced fronts, but behind these the quarters are extremely humble, except in providing a tiny subdivision for use as a study. Such dwellings had to be altered in the nineteenth century to provide, if no more, a genteel approach to the parlour. A parsonage recommended by Isaac Ware in 1756, for a clergyman with a small family, was merely a cottage, one room deep, with a kitchen and wash house in a lean-to at the back.

> Upon the level of the ground, if it be dry and wholesome, may be an entrance from the principal door; and on each side of it a parlour. In front may be the stair-case; and over these lodging rooms. Behind may be placed a kitchen and wash house which need be no more than sheds well covered; and, as most who devote themselves to a country life take the amusements of reading and riding, beyond the right hand parlour may be a study, covered as the kitchen, and beyond to the left a stable.

Parsons were expected to earn something from farming their glebe lands, however brief these might be, it being said that this kept them in touch with agricultural life. The Rev. James Woodforde (occupying a house rather than a cottage) had eight acres of land at Weston Longville in Norfolk, and on 14 September 1776 he noted in his diary:

> Very busy all day with my barley, did not dine till 5 in the after noon, my harvest men dined here today, gave them some beef and some plumb pudding and as much liquor as they would drink. This evening finished my harvest and all carried into the barn.

Later that year, on 3 December, he wrote of having had what he called 'my frolic for my people to pay tithe to me this day. I gave them a good dinner. . . .'

In the second half of the eighteenth century an improved system of agriculture via Enclosures was creating greater tithe values and more profitable glebe farms; and big landowners who had livings to bestow began to regard them as worth the acceptance of a younger son, a brother, or perhaps an ex-tutor, as suitable, indeed, for men of their own class: at Yalding in Kent parsons called Warde are listed as having held the living almost continuously for 200 years. Many landowners strengthened their empires by actually buying up the rights to present an incumbent, known as advowsons, remarking that they wanted a parson who approved of them. Sometimes university colleges introduced to one of their livings a priest who had influence in the senior common room.

Both kinds of patron would undertake to rebuild the parsonage, in the classical manner, or to improve an old one – Shepperton Rectory in Middlesex early acquired a beautiful classical façade in brick on top of sixteenth-century timber framing. Gradually a greater proportion of the parish clergy were graciously housed and fittingly high in the educational and social scale.

An endowed living was seen, like a college fellowship, less as an introduction to duty than as a coveted prize to be enjoyed as a privilege (evangelicanism was not good form), and part of the privilege was having a house that was a cut above the average farmhouse, if not a scaled-down version of a Palladian mansion: clergymen, with notebooks, are said often to have been among the visitors to stately homes, which could be viewed easily in the eighteenth century on payment of a tip to a servant.

Archbishop Cranmer's advice to the clergy to 'content themselves with decency without sumptuousness, lest it awaken envy' was now considered capable of re-interpretation; some parsonages seem to have been expensively adjusted merely to look more imposing to passengers of passing mail coaches. There was a special incentive for a parson to improve his house if it was in a family living, and some spent their own money on this work,

36 A parson seated by the fire in his Georgian parsonage at the end of the eighteenth century. The disposing of curtains appears still to give difficulty. Rowlandson, c. 1810.

if not for the glory of God, at least for the glory of their families. Dr Daniell Phillips was appointed vicar of Much Marcle because of his connection with the Kirles (who were still the patrons of the living in the 1960s) and at once set about building a vicarage worthy of his standing. The back of it can be seen from the Ross–Ledbury road above a rampart of yew; three dormer windows cling to the steep roof and tall sash windows look out of brick walls mellowed by two centuries of sun.

It was not unusual for the new brand of parson to be able to build or enlarge at his own expense. The Rev. Robert Breton added two wings around 1750 to his rectory at Weston-under-

Penyard in Herefordshire and also 'a gallery joining on to the study or new building next to the garden and great parlour'. The Rev. Robert Bradshaw built a new house for himself near the church at Guestling in Sussex: he bequeathed it to the living, providing this on his death in 1736 with two parsonages.

Some well-off parsons liked to arrange to have a parsonage that was not near the church. They did this both to enable them to have lawns and an imposing drive and to avoid bringing up their children almost in a churchyard, with their lives punctuated by funerals and passing bells (the lives of the Brontë children at Haworth were thus troubled). Parson Woodforde visited Sparham in Norfolk in 1779 and found that Parson Attle had built 'a noble house' and that his fields about him 'looked exceeding neat and well'. Woodforde observes: 'He built the house himself and it cost him 1000 pound.' In 1827, 815 parsons were living, for various reasons, about two miles from their church.

With their interest in having prominently sited modern houses, the clergy were influential in spreading Palladian-Renaissance architecture to remote parts of the country. But William Cowper, author of *The Task*, disapproved of certain parsons spending large sums on their houses and wrote in a letter of having just looked at some ruinous churches, which gave him great offence.

> I could not help wishing that the honest vicar, instead of indulging his genius for improvements . . . and converting half an acre of his glebe land into a bowling-green, would have applied part of his income to the more laudable purpose of sheltering his parishioners from the weather during their attendance on divine service. It is no uncommon thing to see the parsonage house . . . in exceeding good repair, while the church perhaps has scarce any other roof than the ivy that grows over it.

The gap between the rich and the poor clergy was considered scandalous by some at the beginning of the Regency period. Half of the 10,000 or so livings still had parsonages that were humble, earth-floored cottages, like Dr Primrose's in *The Vicar of*

37 A parson seemingly wishing to demonstrate, on arrival for a visit, that he is a member of the gentry. The maidservant is being handed his wig for attending to. Rowlandson, c. 1810.

Wakefield, while a most noticeable minority were commodious residences, seeming to reflect clerical affluence. Uncommuted tithes did in truth grow in value with each increase in the price of corn: a quarter cost 43*s*. in 1792 and 126*s*. in 1812. Woodforde received an 'enormous price' for his wheat in 1801, though he had the charity to express the hope that the price would soon fall, for the benefit of the poor.

The Rev. Sydney Smith at least worked with his own hands to achieve a splendid parsonage, designed by himself, at Foston-le-Clay in Yorkshire. 'I live trowel in hand and my whole soul', he wrote, 'is filled by lath and plaster.' He and a few men he had hired tried to bake their own bricks, but, after 150,000 had failed to harden, they decided it would answer better to have them delivered from a distance in carts. His family and the servants moved in before the end of the winter of 1814. Smith had dried the place by having fires burning in every room for two months, keeping them bright by means of air tubes leading into the grates from the outer air: he was ahead of his time in some of his ideas, and preferred, for example, coved to corniced ceilings. Macaulay, a stern critic of parsonages, described the house in 1826 as 'the most commodious and the most appropriate rectory that I ever saw'. Smith: 'I aimed at making it a snug parsonage and I think I have succeeded.'

The more fortunate clergymen's studies grew in size, their interests often going beyond farming and sport. Dean Swift's friend, the Rev. John Geree, though 'living in a little obscure corner of the world called Letcombe near Wantage in Berks', had a 'pretty good study of books in his rectory'. The Rev. Francis Blomefield not only collected a mass of books in the 1750s in the rectory at Fersfield, he also printed there the first volume of his *History of Norfolk*. Dr Alexander Scott, who had been Nelson's Chaplain and brought boxes of books aboard with him, accepted in 1817 the Crown living of Catterick in Yorkshire and was charmed by the accommodation for books in a white, bowfronted rectory. He said in a letter: 'Went to Richmond on Tuesday to buy a horse – went into an old bookshop – bought books and left the horse. Books do not eat anything.'

One of the amenities of the second rectory built by Sydney Smith – that for Combe Florey in Somerset already referred to in chapter 3 – was a study 28 feet long lined with shelves. The books Sydney Smith arranged there were bound in red and blue. Such clergymen could properly talk of their studies as libraries. The Rev. Samuel Parr, vicar of Hatton in Warwickshire for thirtynine years until his death in 1825, had a library of 10,000 volumes and the Rev. Francis Wrangham of Hunmanby in Yorkshire, a library of allegedly 15,000 volumes.

What happened to the Rev. George Jekyll indicated the importance of a study for a country parson. He was appointed to the living of West Coker in Dorset in 1802 and, according to Elizabeth Ham's *Autobiography*,

38 A parson making notes of the arrangements in a squire's parlour. Rowlandson, c. 1810.

whilst he was re-building the parsonage house they were living in a mere cottage where he could not have his books about him, nor even a study to himself. His wife was ignorant and violent, so he was driven abroad to look for comfort. Every night he was at some one or another of the neighbouring farmers and so contracted a habit of low dissipation.

The possibility for some parsons of holding more than one living at once, pluralism, and of living at a distance from their churches, absenteeism, had the effect of ensuring that a large number of the smaller parsonages never received a Georgian front or even ordinary maintenance; for these tended to be let to curates far too poor to spend anything on them. Absenteeism increased in the Regency. Diocesan records show that in 1827 no less than 3,598 incumbents did not live in the parsonage of particular livings, 42 per cent of them giving as their reason 'want or unfitness of the parsonage house'.

The early nineteenth century saw a mania for clerical

building. Some of the parsonages were Gothic now, on the ground that God preferred it, and most no longer resembled superior farmhouses, with barns, because the clergy were ceasing to be farmers. Bishops still made eloquent use of such farming metaphors from the Bible as the Good Shepherd seeking lost sheep in the London slums, but they discouraged their clergy from having more than this verbal contact with agriculture. One bishop, Dr Horsley, said he was shocked to think of clergymen using a scythe and spreading manure on the land. 'The clergy should be kept apart', he told the Lords in 1803, 'from those occupations which would degrade them from the rank they ought to hold in society, and mix them in familiar habits with the inferior orders.'

An Act of 1836 commuted all tithes in kind into rent charges, so that parsons were grudgingly given their tithes in the form of cash by the landowners, and so were spared the squabbles there had been for centuries over such matters as the tenth of a pound of apples. The assured income in cash encouraged even more parsons to undertake home improvements – and enlargements for bigger families. The scale of parsonage building during the ensuing Victorian period, in heavy Gothic and other revived styles, makes it today a pleasure to come upon occasionally an old parsonage which is a placid-looking small, or less-than-small, Georgian house.

The information about particular clergymen in this chapter is almost entirely owed to the research of Mr B. Anthony Bax, the fruits of which appear in his long and most readable book, *The English Parsonage*. I recommend this work especially for the sections about the private lives of the clergy over the centuries.

10

FURNISHING AND LIGHTING

I particularly like the doors: they are always smooth and shut firmly . . . the key is always beautifully made. The chairs and tables are made of mahogany of fine quality and have a brilliant polish like that of finely-tempered steel. (François de la Rochefoucauld, during a long stay at Bury St Edmunds in 1784.)

The compactness of the typical Georgian house plan gives smaller rooms than are suggested by a dignified elevation. Twelve feet by twelve, perhaps fifteen by fifteen, is usual, and present-day occupants may have adjusted matters by throwing two rooms into one.

Contemporary engravings indicate that a lack of space in the dining room, in particular, became oppressive during the long afternoon sessions at the table, a table for which an extra section might have to be carried to and fro. The deep concave front of a tiny new sideboard was designed, Sheraton said, to secure the head servant from the jostles of his assistants.

Throughout the period furnishing in all rooms tended to be sparse; householders considered the visual merits of each piece and tried to give it a suitable setting. The selective room arrangements of Georgian times were in fact much more like modern practice than that of the Victorians, who accepted clutter. Chairs, tables and desks were pushed up against walls, the latter being protected by a dado rail, to leave the maximum of unencumbered space in the middle of the room; and there, on the periphery, such furniture normally remained, beneath pictures marshalled in patterns with the bottoms of their frames forming straight lines. Round tea tables with tripod legs for stability were brought in as needed: not until the Regency period were armchairs and settees allowed to remain permanently gathered round the fireplace.

Interiors tended to rely for their effect, even in modest houses, on architectural treatment. The larger sheets of glass available in the Regency period led to the inclusion of mirrors in the treatment, architects happily noticing that they could give an illusion of extra space; but their architectural use was sometimes

39 Lack of space in the dining room could become oppressive – a small dining room at an inn. After Robert Dighton, 1792.

overdone. Donald Pilcher relates in his book *The Regency Style* that, at a house called Pitzhanger in Ealing, a visitor mistook a pair of enfiladed mirrors for a passage and injured himself so severely that they had to be removed.

Classical shapes and proportions affected craftsmen everywhere, with the result that very few new everyday articles were ill-formed, whether they were kettles, pokers, door handles, knockers or drinking vessels. The interiors of houses seen in the paintings and satirical prints of the time may show ugly human beings, indulging in gluttony, perhaps, or with their wigs askew, but the objects about them are the opposite of ugly.

The sense of sight was a joy to the people of the Georgian period, helping them to ignore these effects of uncleanliness which would today be most distressing. Just give us plenty of beautiful objects, they seem to have thought, and that will compensate for all that is unsavoury.

Some of the unsavoury defects seem quite unnecessary in view of the absence of dust-collecting carpets and often curtains (the owner of a carpet was likely to hang it on a wall), and in view of the ease with which servants could be engaged. But domestic servants tended to be both dirty and lazy. The architect, John Wood senior, wrote in his *Essay Towards a Description of Bath*, 1749, that 'to hide the dirt, the boards of the dining room and most of the other floors in that town were made a brown colour with soot and small beer'.

Standards of housework clearly rose later in the period and François de la Rochefoucauld, who visited England in 1784, said in *Mélanges sur l'Angleterre* that English houses were 'constantly washed inside and out, generally on Saturdays' and that there always seemed to be 'a strip of drugget on the stairs'. He did everything he could to find out 'if this cleanliness was natural to the English' and 'was led to the conclusion that it was only external: everything you see partakes of this most desirable quality, but the English neglect what you are not supposed to see.' It was not expected that the kitchen would be seen. 'The worst thing that could befall you', wrote de la Rochefoucauld, who stayed in numerous houses, 'would be to go into the kitchen

40 A gentleman might not behave well, but every object in his rooms would be pleasingly designed. Gillray, 1792.

before dinner – the dirt is indescribable.'

What house owners did wish to be noticed was that every piece of downstairs furniture was new. It was unfashionable to mix in antiques in the present-day manner: furniture a hundred years old and dating back to James I's reign was heavy and oaken and exactly what no one wished to have on view; and where there was money to buy new, such pieces were got rid of or put in attics. Furniture craftsmen, taking great trouble with the fashioning of a cabriole leg, were inspired by the knowledge that their work would be thoroughly seen. House carpenters making doors and windows and their architraves also looked forward to their work being looked at, and they could not approve the coming, eventually, of a fashion for floor carpets and window curtains. They would have appreciated Cobbett's indignant comment in 1830 about the new-style farmhouse with its *'parlour!* Aye, and a *carpet* and *bell-pull*, too'.

Communications were generally bad till well after the middle of the century and village joiners and village cabinet makers were turned to for house furnishing; these came to supply an ever-wider range of customers with versions of the chairs and tables admired in London. The craftsmen saw them in local big houses, they borrowed and copied them as nearly as they could, they followed instructions in pattern books. Chairs and tables were the main items needed for downstairs rooms, for cupboards of all sorts were being built in. The following brief inventory for an eighteenth-century parlour is typical: 'one table, eight chairs, two stooles'.

Heavy import duties on mahogany were taken off in 1721, and after 1750 this wood, so it is often said, superseded walnut for furniture; it came in large widths, was very strong, carved easily, resisted worm and did not crack or warp. Plenty of walnut furniture went on being made, however, all through the Georgian period, a fact overlooked because, walnut being so perishable compared with oak and mahogany, little survives. In fact, some of the country craftsmen's best work was done in walnut and it remained popular in the provinces in the 1750s. Ralph Fastnedge in *English Furniture Styles* quotes a mid-century

41 A drawing room furnished in the late-eighteenth-century style. From a series of 'Prodigal Son' prints.

letter from a member of the Purefoy family to a chairmaker of Birchester:

> Mr King. As I understand you to make chaires of wallnut tree frames with 4 legs without any barrs for Mr Vaux of Caversfield, if you do such I desire you will come over here in a week's time any morning but Wensday. I shall want about 20 chairs. This will oblige, Your friend to serve you, Elizabeth Purefoy.

The difference between the furnishing of houses in the resort of Bath at the beginning and in the middle of the eighteenth century was described in some detail by John Wood senior – and he, too, refers to chairs and chests of drawers being newly-made in walnut around 1750. In the 1720s, he wrote,

> if the walls of any of the rooms were covered with wainscot, it was with such as was mean and never painted . . . the doors were slight and thin, and the best locks had only iron

coverings varnished: with cane or rush-bottomed chairs the principal rooms were furnished, and each chair seldom exceeded three half crowns in value; nor were the tables, or chests of drawers, better of their kind, the chief being made of oak: the looking glasses were small, mean and few in number; and the chimney furniture consisted of a slight iron fender. . . .

But, as new buildings rose and old ones were improved:

the floors were laid with finest clean deals, or Dutch oak boards; the rooms were all wainscotted and painted in a costly and handsome manner; marble slabs, and even chimney pieces, became common; the doors in general were not only made thick and substantial, but they had the best sort of brass lock put on them; walnut tree chairs, some with leather, and some with damask or worked bottoms supplied the place of such as were seated with cane or rushes; the oak tables and chests of drawers were exchanged, the former for such as were made of mahogany, the latter for such as were made either with the same wood, or with walnut tree; handsome glasses were added to the dressing tables, nor did the proper chimneys or peers of any of the rooms long remain without framed mirrours of no inconsiderable size; and the furniture of every chief chimney was composed of a brass fender, with tongs, poker and shovel agreable to it.

Although furniture was thinly distributed, little of it creeping out into the centre of rooms until the Regency, there came to be an abundance of china ornaments in small houses as their occupiers decided to copy the proprietors of the great houses. Daniel Defoe wrote that it was Queen Mary, wife of William III, who 'brought in the custom or humour, as I may call it, of furnishing houses with china-ware, which increased to a strange degree afterwards, people piling their china upon the tops of cabinets scrutoirs and every chimney-piece to the tops of ceilings, and even setting up shelves for their china-ware.'

'My sister', wrote Lady Elizabeth in 1735, 'is become China mad, frequents all the shops in town in order to gett old or Dresden china. The first purchases she made of that sort of ware were yellow and green tea cups, variously and most hideously intermingled as like Delf as ever was seen, but they told her 'twas old china and that was inducement enough to her to buy 'em. However, they are now exchanged for a set of Dresden.' This quotation was found in the Chatsworth manuscripts by Mrs Burton, author of *The Georgians at Home*.

At the start of the eighteenth century, the china put on display was either glazed pottery or a porcelain of the soft-paste kind. Vain attempts to find out the Chinese art of porcelain-making had been going on for a century when, in 1709, true, hard-paste porcelain was achieved at Meissen, near Dresden. It was not satisfactorily manufactured in England until around the 1750s.

Among ornaments for which England's Georgian era was famous are the figures. 'Un-paper the curtains, take the covers off the couch and chairs, and put the china figures on the mantelpiece immediately', Mrs Heidelburg tells her parlour-maid in *The Clandestine Marriage*, when a visitor approaches. All classes liked a princess who was disguised as a shepherdess and shown being wooed in floral surroundings by an elegant shepherd; a pretty lady in a chair attended by a black page and having beside her a round tea table holding a chocolate pot and cups.

When chimney stacks retreated to just inside the walls, instead of projecting from them, the resultant alcoves on each side of the fireplace made (as they still do) favourite places for cabinets or shelves of china. At night the flames of an open fire helped to illuminate the ornaments.

The Georgian age was almost innocent of pollution by oil lamps. It was still an age of candles and, for the poor, of rushes dipped in mutton fat called rush lights. And, despite the importance of candles for artificial light, these were far less efficient than the candles of today. The tallow kind became unfashionable, but Georgian composites of sperm oil and coconut oil mixed with tallow had the disadvantage of containing glycerine, which burns badly. Cheap candles known as dips were sold in one-pound bunches tied by the wicks and looking like bananas; they burned no worse than the neater, more expensive, moulded candles. Eventually a French chemist discovered how to remove glycerine and his Star candles, introduced in 1831, were sought after.

Candles might be made to do a lot of work, as when they were massed in chandeliers (ladies with the once-fashionable tall hair style, eighteen inches or so high, had to be careful of fire), and the rise of a flourishing china industry was matched by new uses for glass in lighting equipment. As early as 1714, candle-holding 'glass shandeliers' were advertised in the *London Gazette*. Such chandeliers, with cut glass drops, were usually called lustres. One maker, William Watkinson, in 1727 called them fire lustres. Approving this term, Mrs Burton has written that 'the beauty, the sparkle, the shimmering rainbow and jewel-like colours of the chandelier are now largely lost in the steady, unwavering light of the electric bulb. The real beauty of a fire lustre can only be seen in the tentative, flickering flames of innumerable candles.'

Some watercolour drawings by John Harden show almost photographically what rooms in a modest-sized house in the Lake District looked like at the end of the Georgian period. The rooms have people busy in them and using pieces of furniture moved for the purpose from their accustomed positions; clearly, being near the fire brings more light for reading as well as more warmth. No lamps are seen. It was, however, now possible to buy an invention known as the peg lamp which smokily burned whale oil (a flat instead of a round wick was found to cause less smoke), and an improved lamp, the glass globed Argand, which burned colza seed oil and had an air burner.

As for lighting the fires and the candles, it is a strange truth about Georgian domestic life that until about 1805 the best way known was still by means of tinder and flint. The operation – with false starts – could last half an hour, and is ably described in Gareth Adamson's *Machines at Home*. A length of steel with a serrated edge was struck sharply on a lump of flint above some tinder, which usually consisted of dry cotton cloth. In due course

42 A Regency trio sketched from life, showing the furniture in use
and a young man reading aloud. Pen and wash by John Harden,
1827.

43 A single candle illuminating the evening occupations of four people. Pen and wash by John Harden, 1804.

a spark fell on the tinder and set it smouldering. Now the smouldering fragment was coaxed to set light to a sliver of pinewood which had been dipped in sulphur to make it burn readily, and with luck the match would burn long enough to light a candle resting in a socket on the lid of the tinder box. A damper was applied to the tinder to stop it smouldering.

In 1805 matches more like those of today were invented. Known as bottle matches, they consisted of slivers of wood treated with potash, sugar and gum – as well as with sulphur – and they lit when they were dipped into a bottle containing concentrated sulphuric acid in asbestos fibre. Matches which burst into flame simply on being struck were invented in 1829 by a chemist of Stockton-on-Tees called John Walker. These were Lucifers. A fold of sandpaper was needed to make them strike.

It was not until almost the middle of the nineteenth century that matches were made to ignite with a harmless form of phosphorus; a Swedish firm put the material on the boxes, not on the matches, thereby supplying the world with safety matches which would not strike on anything but the outside of the box. By this time the (more easily lighted) oil and gas lamps were illuminating, in many houses, modern furniture which demonstrated to the discerning, as they looked about them during evening visits, that the Georgian classical tradition in furniture design was fast fading away entirely in favour of designs with a romantic, old English appeal. J. C. Loudon approved the change, and his great and popular *Encyclopaedia* on furnishings had helped to influence the trade. He admired in particular the sharply pointed angles of Gothic architecture and, in encouraging the introduction of these into furniture (often as mere trivial ornament), he had guilelessly helped to make Gothic the commercially successful fashion which hastened the descent of furniture design into ill-proportioned showiness.

11

BEDROOMS

Bedrooms, known as chambers, were even more sparsely furnished than sitting rooms and could be so cold, with draughts piercing uncovered floor boards, that a lot of people in effect did not sleep in them: they slept in a stuffy, compact room within a room, in a curtained four-post bed. Such beds were by no means rare outside the houses of the rich, for they are described again and again in the inventories of modest eighteenth-century farmhouses.

At the beginning of the Georgian period an effort was made to give beds (and bedroom chairs) a warm and inviting appearance, and the wooden framework, with posts, head and canopy, would be completely covered with fabric. Celia Fiennes in her *Journeys* describes the main bedroom of 'a neate house' at Epsom, seen in 1702. It was

> hung with very rich tapestry, the bed crimson damaske lined with white India satin with gold and crimson flowers
> printed, the chairs, one red damaske the other crostitch very rich. . . .

John Wood senior wrote of Bath that the ladies of the city, with their daughters and maids, flowered the bed coverings 'with worsted during the intervals between the seasons to give the beds a gaudy look'.

By the middle of the eighteenth century the bed was lower (previously a set of steps was resorted to by some for getting in); the curtains were less voluminous and the wooden framework had become visible. The canopy part, known as a tester – it was firmly supported by the bedhead at the back and by columns at the front – now sometimes had a frieze and cornice recalling the proportions of one or other of the classical orders of architecture. The pair of columns recalled them, too, in a rather attenuated way. In fashioning these columns Georgian bed-joiners wished to show the chair-makers that they were equally familiar with the orders and their correct proportions (these were in fact illustrated in every workman's pattern book), and that they knew how to take discreet liberties for the sake of a decorative effect.

Inside, the four-posters were furnished with sheets and a large

44   Four-post bed of about 1740.

feather quilt on a springless base. The great thing was to keep out cold air. The tent bed, doing this as effectively as the four-poster, got its name from its resemblance, when the curtains were drawn, to a gabled tent. The tent beds were seldom made large enough for two. According to one of Horace Walpole's letters, a newly married Countess of Coventry, staying the night at Calais in 1752, was offered a tent bed by Lord Downe who thought the inn beds were infested, but she refused it. 'I had rather be bit to death', she wrote home, 'than lie one night from my dear Cov.'

Beds were very difficult to keep clean in Georgian times, and laments and advice on this matter appear regularly, as Mrs Burton has noted, in the household books and journals of the age of elegance. Madame Johnson wrote in *The Young Woman's Companion* in 1765:

> Set open the windows of bedchambers and uncover the beds
> to sweeten them; which will be a great help against bugs
> and fleas. . . . Spunge with a mixture of spirits of wine, spirit
> of turpentine and camphire.

Bed-bugs remained a trouble well beyond the Georgian period (it is made clear in Mr Wright's book *Clean and Decent*), and not only in the small houses where few servants were kept. No objection seems to have been raised at Buckingham Palace when Tiffin & Son put up their advertisement:

TIFFIN & SON
Bug-destroyers to Her Majesty

The senior partner of this firm was interviewed by Henry Mayhew, chronicler of London life, and told him that he worked for the upper classes only.

> I was once at work on the Princess Charlotte's own bedstead. I was in the room and she asked me if I had found anything, and I told her no; but just at that moment I *did* happen to catch one, and upon that she sprang up on the bed, and put her hand on my shoulder, to look at it.

Tiffin's was not the first firm to do this work for the Royal Family. Andrew Cooke of Holborn Hill mentioned that he had done it in an advertisement for his services in 1775; also that in various houses he had 'cured 16,000 beds'. Mary Southall of Southwark, another bed-bug destroyer, was willing to wait on 'Such quality and gentry as are troubled with buggs' and also prepared to help those lower in the socio-financial scale.

> Persons who cannot afford to pay her price, and is willing to destroy them themselves, may by sending notice to her place of abode, be furnished with the NON PAREIL LIQUOR, &c.

The bedrooms of small Georgian inns tended to be bare-boarded rooms whose bedding was so unpleasant that the wise traveller took his own sheets with him. John Byng repeatedly describes in his diaries the poor state of English inn bedrooms and the horror of having forgotten to bring sheets, and William Combe's famous character Dr Syntax is aroused one night at an inn by the bustling sound of rats mauling his wig on the floor.

It was the universal custom for men to wear horsehair wigs in the eighteenth century, a custom extending to artisans and many labourers, and the bedroom or its closet was the natural place for combing and dressing them and sprinkling on powder. And just as farthingales and hooped skirts led to wider chairs to accommodate the sitter, so wig-wearing caused cabinet makers to make wig blocks and wig stands for use in the bedroom. The wig block was a head represented in wood and leather, with a brief circular-based stand, for holding a wig to be dressed; a wig stand was a small turned baluster, finishing in a bulbous knob, which made somewhere to hang up one's wig at night.

It so happens that today the term wig stand is often wrongly applied to another bedroom article, the light tripod stand with small drawers whose function was to hold a wash basin. Whether on such a stand or on something more substantial, Georgian wash basins were only large enough for a perfunctory dabble, but they at least left room for the paints and powders used by both men and women.

The size of wash basins did not trouble people, not because they had a bigger wash with a portable bath in their bedrooms, but because they preferred to attend to themselves by putting on strong-smelling essences. These did not always work, as Lord Hervey makes very clear in his *Memoirs*. But even the face was not washed much. An etiquette book of 1782 said water made the face 'too sensitive' and that it should be 'wiped each morning with white linen'.

Elegant bedside pot cupboards with a drawer, reflecting prototypes by Hepplewhite and Sheraton, began to appear in the more genteel small houses at the end of the eighteenth century. They were sometimes called night tables instead, neither term, unlike commode, being ambiguous. A commode was a very grand type of chest of drawers only seen in grand houses, and because of its smart associations the name was applied by the trade to every box on legs with a pot beneath the lid: these were called night commodes, soon shortened by users to just commodes. They became usual in small-house bedrooms, where they spared blushes and gave enough insulation to prevent the winter freezing-up under the bed noted in 1785 by Parson Woodforde.

Shortening of terms is of course responsible for the pot within a commode being called a chamber (the old word for bedroom) rather than chamber pot. The better kind, for use without a box, was of earthenware rather than metal throughout the Georgian period. Around the 1750s the Potteries found a market for almost aggressively ornamental chambers in white porcelain, decorated with colour, and later on they sold thousands with flowers in full relief on the outside and a frog inside, or even a representation of the dreaded Napoleon.

12

HYGIENE

Georgian houses were easier to plan than later kinds, being quite uncomplicated by fixed baths, sanitary conveniences and plumbing. Georgian ladies left withdrawing rooms to 'pluck a rose' in the garden and really did something else veiled by a hooped skirt, a procedure which Jonathan Swift in his satirical pamphlet *Directions to Servants* (1731, published 1745) pretended was the best possible; he was offended by some ladies' use of 'an odious implement' indoors; servants should impose a corrective by doing their slop work flamboyantly.

Swift's point about the garden, assuming a large one, is almost acceptable, but many town houses had only small patches and it was consequently usual for pails to be emptied from upper windows. References by the contemporary writers Smollett and James Boswell suggest that the people of Edinburgh long continued primitive in this matter and even in 1832 Exeter was said to have open gutters as the only means of disposing of household slops. S. S. Hellyer said in his book *Plumbing* that the traditional warning, 'Gardez l'eau' was not always given there and that 'when people went into the streets at night it was necessary, to avoid disagreeable accidents from the windows, that they should take with them a guide who, as he went along, called out with a loud voice "Haud yer han".' However, Edinburgh did have men whose business it was 'to perambulate the streets carrying conveniences [pails] suspended from a yoke on their shoulders, and enveloped by cloaks sufficiently large to cover both their appliance and customers'.

The best kind of sanitation for small Georgian houses was an outside privy, also referred to as Jericho or the necessary house, with a cesspit just below the seat. (The earth closet, most satisfactory when properly managed, was a post-Georgian invention.) Parson Woodforde in April 1780 wrote in his diary of painting some boarding 'put up to prevent people in the kitchen seeing those who had occasion to go to Jericho'. At some parsonages, according to Mr Anthony Bax, the privy would be masked by a yew tree which kept it cool in summer and less cold in winter. Artistry was sometimes shown in the design of the building: it might be made to resemble a garden temple or have a typical Georgian façade in mellow brick. A privy would often be provided with seats of several sizes, not necessarily for the whole family to use at one time, but rather to ensure that children did not fall through.

In a heavily built-up part of a town, the privy might be indoors, with the cesspit possibly just below a sitting room floor. Lawrence Wright gives numerous details about these matters in *Clean and Decent*. On underfloor cesspits, he quoted a story from W. Eassie's *Sanitary Arrangements for Dwellings*, 1874, concerning a plumber who held a lighted candle as he raised flagstones by a kitchen sink and was blown up. Below was the cesspit, which had not been disturbed for many years.

The conscientious householder arranged for cesspits under his backyard or house to be emptied regularly by the night men, the nature of whose work with buckets and carts had not changed since the time of Pepys. At the start of the Georgian period the value to farms of the sewage made it worth their while to have it carted out of town, but as London grew the trips became uneconomical and the buckets were instead carried to communal cesspools, or to a river – which also provided drinking water. London's River Fleet was not recognized as a sewer and covered in until 1841.

The worst feature of these later arrangements was contamination of drinking water, which would bring fatal illness to the best houses. Cruelly sited cesspools leaked into the ground, and so did the few rudimentary brick sewers designed to convey slops to rivers. Yet everywhere in town and country people had wells. It was common for every kind of cesspit to be covered over when full and then forgotten when a new one was dug. At a particular Georgian house in the country, attention was drawn to a forgotten pit, Mr Wright says, by the sudden sinking of a carriage on reaching the front door.

The Georgian sanitary arrangements of mansions were hardly more efficient, let alone safer, than those of small houses, and they failed to improve steadily in the Victorian period: as late as 1861 Prince Albert died of typhus at Windsor, where fifty-three inadequate cesspits were then found beneath the floors.

Water closets of a kind were being put together early in the eighteenth century, and examples are still to be seen at a few of the stately homes open to the public; but at no time were they installed anywhere as a matter of course. Kedleston, Syon House and Osterley have one each, looking like afterthoughts in niches of reception rooms; none was indicated by William Kent in his plans for Holkham – where the dining room is 200 feet from the kitchen – and a plan of sewers and drains in Isaac Ware's *The Complete Body of Architecture* makes provision only for outside lavatories. Bad smells in a house in themselves harmed no one, disease organisms coming by way of food that was physically contaminated; but although many thought they were harmful, the function of an outside ventilation pipe in keeping the air sweet was not appreciated till far into the nineteenth century.

For the few who were interested in water-aided sanitation there was, first, the pan closet in which a hinged metal pan, when level, kept a few inches of water at the bottom of an upper bowl of earthenware. On pulling up a handle in the mahogany casing, the pan swung down and discharged into a lower cast iron receiver connected to a primitive drain. Offensively, the receiver was also a kind of retainer. Pan closets were nevertheless on the market, among others, throughout Queen Victoria's reign. Hellyer wrote in 1890 that, despite some improvements, 'it remains to this day the most insanitary closet in use' and that 'the only bliss that the public can have about so foul a thing is ignorance of its nature'. Many continued to be used in the twentieth century, including thousands which were exported to the USA. A second and only slightly more efficient water closet of the eighteenth century was the plunger closet, in which a leather-faced plug was lowered to close the outlet but in practice did not long stay watertight.

A mains supply of often lethal water reached certain streets of London and of other centres around the mid-eighteenth century. It was an intermittent supply. Houses connected received water for two or three hours on about three days a week, when theoretically tanks would be filled. Ball valves, coming in during the 1740s, spared a servant from having to remember to open his main tap and from the consequences of not turning it off.

In 1756 Dr Lucas wrote in *An Essay on Waters* that London was served with 'simple water' in greater abundance than any other city in Europe. César de Saussure, a Swiss, noticed this, too, and said in a letter, 'But would you believe it . . . absolutely none is drunk.' (His letters were published in *A Foreign View of England.*) Numerous people did have the sense not to drink untreated water, and one of the reasons for the popularity of tea, the leaves being used several times by the poor, was that it hid unpleasant tastes lingering in the thoroughly boiled water. Beer was widely recommended; it was served in hospitals and in institutions for charity children.

The main sources for London's piped supply, according to Dr Lucas, were the Thames (at London Bridge, Chelsea and York Buildings), New River, Hampstead Pond and a spring at the end of Rathbone Place – at the latter point it was raised by a 'machine wrought by a horse'. Dr Lucas tested samples by boiling and weighing the residue: Thames water left $16\frac{1}{2}$ grains but there were 90 in the water from Hampstead Pond and 100 in that from the spring at Rathbone Place.

Although water was in short supply by modern standards, scarcity alone cannot justify the exiguous size of the washbasins mentioned in the previous chapter, for which stands were not supplied till about 1750. Floors were scrubbed and soap employed for the job, but the Georgians had little interest in soap and water for cleaning themselves. When they did wash all over, the same little basins were used.

De la Rochefoucauld looked inside English kitchens and observed:

> Women are usually employed and are as black as coal; their arms bared to the elbow, are disgustingly dirty; to save time, they handle the portions of food with their hands . . . you will not see a couple of napkins or dish-cloths, and if you do see one in use, you will have no desire to wipe your hands on it.

Portable baths, copper ones, were rarities. Even St George's

Hospital in London had only one bath at the end of the eighteenth century – and apparently it was not used. The London Hospital had a single bath, too, and kept it in a cellar. Mr Wright quotes a doctor writing in the year 1801 that 'most men resident in London and many ladies, though accustomed to wash their hands and faces daily, neglect washing their bodies from year to year'.

Only one plumbed-in arrangement for washing the body was built in the whole Georgian period. The Lord Mayor of London for the year 1812 did try to have a shower bath fitted at the Mansion House, but the Common Council rejected his request on the ground that 'the want thereof has never been complained of', and Queen Victoria, when she came to the throne in 1837, found no kind of bathroom at Buckingham Palace – although plans had been drawn up for conveying hot water to a portable bath in her bedroom. Elsewhere, however, the Queen could point to ownership of the only existing plumbed-in bath: it was George IV's bath at the Royal Pavilion in Brighton and, measuring sixteen feet by ten, it looked like a small swimming pool. The Queen had it demolished after a time, and its white marble was sawn up to make mantelpieces for Buckingham Palace.

Although people of the Georgian period apparently dragged their feet for so long over personal hygiene, local authorities of a kind did come into being around the middle of the eighteenth century and a tenuous regard for cleanliness which grew up was enough to cause a significant drop in the deaths of children in infancy.

Local authorities were born when the industrial towns ceased to be overgrown villages and were plainly tight-packed towns: the lack of local government and local administration became unbearable, as J. H. Plumb has put it, even to a people who loathed any restraint on their liberty of action. Westminster began the new movement, between 1761 and 1765, when a body of enterprising citizens secured Private Acts of Parliament by which they were enabled to levy a house rate in return for providing cleaning-up services. By the end of the eighteenth century all important streets had common sewers, according to

Simond. 'The drains preclude that awkward process by which necessaries are emptied in Paris, poisoning the air of whole streets, during the night, with effluvia hurtful and sometimes fatal to the inhabitants.' A few rich houses had 'what are called water closets', constantly washed by 'a cistern in the upper story filled with rain water'. Simond watched workmen taking up decayed wooden pipes for water from beneath Oxford Street and Holborn and substituting cast iron tubes which seemed to him extremely large. They were 'upwards of two feet in diameter, branching out down the side streets, into pipes of the diameter of six inches' and Simond observes: 'The water must acquire a ferruginous quality in its passage through so much iron. I think glass pipes might be made. . . .'

The slow growth of local authorities is the most important social development in the second half of the eighteenth century, and one to which attention is seldom drawn. Unlikely though it now seems, in the Regency period both London and certain provincial towns were the wonders of Europe for cleanliness and orderly living.

Those who lived in small houses gained as much as the rich, for most of the diseases of filth were checked, if not destroyed. In the 1790s, for the first time, the birth rate in London passed the death rate. Some years later, with the introduction of bad water-borne sewage arrangements, undue deaths once more became yearly more numerous. Typhoid had come back. But, as Dr Plumb has written, every new development seemed to aid life instead of death. The improved food, the use of pottery instead of pewter, the widespread wearing of cheap cotton clothes, the provision of treated water, the removal of refuse from streets, the foundation of hospitals and a slightly increased knowledge of medicine all contributed to create a rapidly expanding population.

13

THE SASH WINDOW

The sliding sash window early became the hallmark of Georgian houses, its mere proportions giving them their distinctive character and restfulness. Hinged wooden casements, costing half as much, were also used, but sash windows had so many advantages practically and in looks that they became everyone's ideal and would even be fitted to underground coal cellars.

By the middle of the eighteenth century, owners of old timber-framed houses were busy all over the country ripping out small leaded casements and putting in tall sash windows. Sometimes a building would be structurally weakened in the process; or front-room windows would sprout awkwardly from the floor; often a whole new façade had to be built. The energy with which such work was carried out indicates clearly both the desire to conform and dissatisfaction with traditional hinged windows, the latter being seen as incorrigibly vernacular when shut, and awkward, catching the wind, when open.

The double-sash window design, incorporating balance

45   Pre-Georgian windows with leaded panes in iron, hinged casements. Top: mullioned triple light. Bottom: mullioned and transomed double light – the total opening being here of suitable proportions for replacing with a sash window.

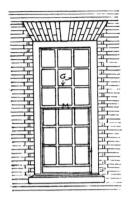 

46   A classical and a Gothic window. Left: early sash window with
the sashes meeting at M and thick glazing bars, G. The frame is
only just set back from the face of the wall; arch and jambs are
picked out in bright pink, gauged brick. Right: late Georgian Gothic
casement window, pointed with tracery work and having a drip
mould above.

weights and lines moving over pulleys, was introduced from
Holland towards the end of the seventeenth century. A few of the
windows had been fitted in Paris, the name coming from the
French word *chassis*, but Holland is the only European country
besides Britain which still has them in quantity: in Holland a
short and generally immovable top sash (*a chassis dormant*) and a
very tall bottom sash is preferred to the British convention, which
seems more pleasing to the eye, of having the two sashes of equal
size.

It is believed that sash windows were first made in England for
the Duke of Lauderdale in 1673. They were used in large
numbers at Chatsworth between 1676 and 1680, at the
Banqueting Hall in Whitehall in 1685 and, during the next five
years, at Windsor Castle, Kensington Palace and Hampton
Court. Partly as a result of royal example, sash windows became
standard for new houses in the Home Counties before the death
of William IV. They spread gradually to other parts of the

country, although some small villages everywhere still had none at the start of the nineteenth century.

Their introduction at Dodsworth Green near Barnsley was noted in John Hobson's journal in 1726: 'Guest [a glazier] put glass into the sash windows in the buttery, being the first that ever was in this town.' (The entry has been quoted by Mrs Burton.) Celia Fiennes was, however, sufficiently aware of them in the year 1698 to observe about Bretby Park in Derbyshire that 'none of the windows are sashes, which in my opinion is the only thing it wants to render it a complete building'.

The woodwork was in those days massive throughout, the groove for the weight worked out of solid wood; but for many small-house windows no weights were supplied and, as a further economy, only the bottom sash moved up and down: it was kept at the required height by means of notches.

To the surprise of Samuel Johnson, utility sash windows had reached the Hebrides in the 1770s. When he wrote about them in *Journey to the Western Isles of Scotland*, he was perhaps thinking that a window represented more than the definition he had given in his *Dictionary*, 'an aperture in a building by which air and light are intromitted':

> Their windows do not move upon hinges, but are pushed up and down in grooves, yet they are seldom accommodated with weights and pulleys. He that would have his window open must hold it with his hand unless, what may be sometimes found among good contrivers, there be a nail which he may stick into a hole to keep it from falling.

An accident involving a falling sash is brutally described by Laurence Sterne in *Tristram Shandy*, 1767. The hero's nurse, to save herself the trouble of fetching the little boy a pot, places him on a seat by the window with one hand and with the other lifts the bottom sash. 'Cannot you contrive, master?', she begs, and just as he is about to do so, 'down came the sash like lightening.'

A humble sash window with no such risk had glazed sections sliding in grooves from side to side, an invention which is thought to have originated in Yorkshire. Plenty of Yorkshire sliding

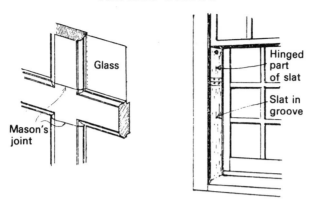

Glass

Mason's
joint

Hinged
part
of slat

Slat in
groove

47   Details of the early sash window. Left: a way of joining bars.
Right: a device for holding lower sash open.

sashes were installed in country parts throughout the eighteenth
century and beyond; they certainly allowed ventilation in a high
wind; but they were inclined to stick in their grooves.

Except for attic windows (these were generally casements), all
frames for up-and-down sash windows were taller than they were
broad. The breadth was taken as the proportioning module. In
grander houses the reception rooms on top of the ground floor
would have windows twice as tall as they were broad; those below
would be shorter to suggest strength. The window heights for
ordinary small houses – as Mr Dan Cruikshank has explained –
were either one and a quarter, one and a half, or one and three-
quarters times the breadth. In general, windows tended to get
taller until, during the Regency, a large tall window was
preferred to two smaller ones with a pier between them. James
Malton wrote in *Designs for Villas*, 1802, of the cheerfulness of 'a
sufficiency of light flowing in from the centre'.

Each pane of glass in a Georgian window was a scaled-down
version not of the whole window but of the shape made by three
quarters of the window height by its breadth. Glazing bars, at
first flat and heavy, grew ever more slender until they became so
thin as to look too fragile: some of the Regency bars were in fact
made of metal.

So great was the appeal of sash windows (with a proper

balancing mechanism) that even the owners of Stuart houses with robust mullions and carefully-made metal casements took the trouble to modernize, a proceeding which was the easier in large Renaissance houses because tall window openings, introduced by Inigo Jones, were already suitable in shape for sash windows. Largely for that reason, few seventeenth-century casements survive.

Mr Clifton-Taylor has set out three reasons for his view that Stuart houses were always aesthetically improved by the substitution of sashes for casements: (1) The typical Stuart window is bisected down the middle and is therefore a duality. (2) An array of casements which are opened is only a little less disturbing than a house hung with flags. (3) White-painted wooden glazing bars, enclosing panes considerably larger than the earlier leaded lights, are bold enough to make a positive contribution to the elevation.

On looking at the front of a small Georgian house, it is not too much to say that the whole design falls into place round the arrangement of windows, doing this well or badly according to the designer's or builder's sense of proportion. In other types of house the windows may seem only incidental features.

People said the sash windows were cheerful, the panes seeming to twinkle and smile in sunlight. And much of their attraction today derives from the slightly wavy surface of the crown glass that was used. This was blown with a pipe. The pipe was dipped into molten glass, withdrawn with a lump of it on the end, blown and rapidly revolved against a wooden bat until the lump of glass spread into a round disc between three and four feet in diameter. The disc was always thicker towards the centre and, right in the middle, where the pipe had been, was a lump known as the bull's eye. For Georgian windows, only selected parts of the disc were cut. Extra skill in the business was brought in by French glass makers who came to England after 1685, when the Revocation of the Edict of Nantes reduced the freedom of Protestants in France. In 1691 an advertiser in the *London Gazette* claimed that his Crown Windsor glass even exceeded French glass.

Shop windows had to be small-paned like the house windows.

48 Late Georgian windows. Above: a triple light bow window.
Below: barrel windows as often used for shops.

Plate glass, had it been invented, would no doubt have been
welcomed by some shopkeepers; others may have realized that
their windows had what Mr Gloag has called the allure of
peepshows; 'the goods within were enhanced by the surprise of
intimate discovery; the eye enjoyed searching out the articles so
pleasantly framed in the panes of glass'. These shop windows
were especially inviting when they jutted out a little and could be
seen from three sides: de la Rochefoucauld enthused about this
kind in one of his letters from England in 1784.

The achievements of the Georgian window makers are the
more remarkable for taking place with a window tax in force.
This tax was first imposed in 1697 and levied on the openings of
all houses having more than six windows, and being worth more
than £5 a year. In the House of Commons in 1747 an
unsuccessful attempt was made to repeal 'a system of collecting

taxes on air and light': far from being repealed, the tax was increased on four separate occasions between 1747 and 1808. It was at last reduced in 1825, but not finally repealed until 1851.

One effect was to encourage the building of detached houses with no windows at the sides and looking like slices taken from a terrace, and another to make it a common practice to block up windows in the manner of the innkeeper's wife in Henry Fielding's novel *Tom Jones* of 1749: 'It is a dreadful thing', she exclaimed, 'to pay as we do. Why now, there is about forty shillings for window lights, and yet we have stopt up all we could; we have almost blinded the house, I am sure.'

Blocked windows, sometimes with painting to simulate what should have been there, are still to be seen on Georgian houses all over Britain. Not quite all were filled in by householders determined to reduce their taxes at the expense of darker rooms: some were blocked from the time of building, for such was the importance attached to the window as an element in a façade that depressions would be made in brand new houses, depressions complete with sill and architrave, so that the harmony of the design should be preserved. Builders could explain to the customer that places had been left for him to fit windows, if he ever cared to pay the extra tax, or if the tax were to be abolished.

Some windows, no doubt, were blocked for reasons of comfort rather than money. In the middle of the century the Rev. William Cole of Bletchley stopped up the third window of his second best bedroom (it looked onto the churchyard) because of there 'being too much light'.

Shortly before the window tax ended it was discovered that, by means of cylinders, thin glass could be made cheaply in huge sheets, and in the 1840s owners of Georgian houses decided that stretches of unbroken glass would give them more light and clearer views. They zealously tore out glazing bars. Who can blame them? There was a new invention to be made use of, an invention on a par with the non-loadbearing wall of the present century which architects have taken advantage of to develop the metal-framed window.

Yet old windows deprived of their glazing bars are dark and

gloomy voids. Inside the house, the character of the rooms is changed. During the Victorian period many house owners began to realize this and had each sash bisected down the middle, but the uneasy duality thus produced gave an even worse appearance. Although the inhabitants of Bath itself, one of Britain's foremost Georgian towns, have been lax about re-attending to their windows, in numerous places it may be found out that glazing bars have been put back into windows too long without them. Most who think about it will agree with the comment of Mr Clifton-Taylor that 'anyone who restores missing glazing bars is performing a service both to himself and to his fellows'. One notable example of this service has been appreciated at Chatsworth, in its south front.

Sash windows are not only still being made, there is a slowly increasing demand for them in both Britain and America. Apart from aesthetic considerations, a number of practical advantages are apparent. For a start, the window cleaner need never use a ladder or a suspended basket, or be tempted to stand on an outside sill – sash windows can be cleaned easily and with safety from within.

The popular picture window does provide householders with an uninterrupted view of the world, but it also provides the public with an uninterrupted view of them. The glinting panes of a sub-divided window, such as the sash, make it impossible for passers-by to take in at a glance the whole of the interior of a downstairs room.

One long-overlooked advantage of sash windows over those that extend themselves along a wall is better resistance to solar radiation which, once in, cannot escape. The effect in sunny weather is especially noticeable in the Northern Hemisphere, where the hottest rays of the sun strike walls: in the Tropics they come from directly overhead and strike the roofs of the buildings, whose walls may be protected by verandas. Tall sash windows break the path of the sun as it moves across a wall, the very wood of the glazing bars having a degree of insulating effect.

A recent survey of two hundred new office blocks brought complaints from nearly half of those who worked in them about summer discomfort through an excess of radiant heat from the sun. On one of the hottest days in 1975, I took the temperature in certain sash-windowed offices and compared it with the temperature in offices whose outer walls were nearly all glass: the sash-windowed rooms were on average seven degrees cooler. I cannot fairly suggest that in winter, without artificial heating, such rooms would be seven degrees warmer, but it is plain that on a cold day a large area of single-thickness glass has a refrigerating effect.

Since the early 1950s architects have thought much in terms of steel-skeleton construction and metal window frames, and they have copied one another in designing unsuitable and disproportionately large windows for modest houses. Some continue to point to the better view made possible, even though on certain days it may be just a huge view of a cold grey sky, which takes away from the feeling of being snugly indoors and sheltered.

A majority does not agree with these architects, if another recent survey may be relied on. The finding was that the acceptability of any view has nothing to do with the area of glass through which it is seen. However, the shape of that area does seem to be of consequence, since most people like to be able to see more than the upper or middle part of such an object as a tree. While a horizontal window generally makes this difficult, a sash window may allow a tree to be seen from the roots up – and a neighbour from slippers to hair as he stands at his front door across the street. The British have had the sense to keep their sash windows for over 200 years. It seems likely that, for one reason or another, they will continue to do so.

14

CHIMNEYS AND FIREPLACES

In the present century many Georgian chimney stacks have been stripped of their chimney pots – usually with advantage visually and without the least setback to the performance of grates. But although the pots may look incongruous against the clean lines of a classical house, only some were in fact Victorian additions.

No chimney pots at all were used by the great chimney builders of the Stuart period. They have no function that cannot be achieved without them and merely reduce flue openings at the top and provide the wind with a slight edge to blow across, instead of a completely flat plane.

Almost unknown before the eighteenth century, they were first used on the slender stacks which rose on each side of hipped roofs, unsupported from eaves level upwards; fearful of making these stacks too tall (many today lean), builders fitted pots to gain the height necessary to avoid downdraughts and smoking fires. Nevertheless a craze for them set in, and under George III everyone seemed to want them. Constable depicts chimney pots in his pictures *The Haywain* and *A Cornfield with Figures* and in a drawing of Fitzroy Square in London.

It is apparent that some Georgian craftsmen had their own idea about what to do with the chimney pots they were expected as a matter of course to fit. They pushed them down into the stack so that only an inch protruded and no part of them was visible from ground level. The practice is still sometimes followed today. Meanwhile, for those interested in these pots as antiques, the Rev. Valentine Fletcher published in 1968 a charming illustrated monograph on their history called *Chimney Pots and Stacks*.

Palladio's chimneys in Italy had been just tubes put almost anywhere (but unobtrusively) and Georgian builders, as though following him in this, took far less interest in the construction of chimneys than their predecessors. But whatever the inadequacy of some Georgian chimney stacks, leading to present-day dampness in bedroom ceilings, much attention was devoted to beautifying the fireplaces they served. These were a focal point of social life, a source of light as well as warmth.

How to treat fireplaces was a matter of perplexity to the early designers of classical houses in England. Plainly, such important

49 Chimney development. Georgian builders, seemingly following Palladio, came to take scant interest in the construction of chimney stacks. Left: brick chimney of 1600 (no pots). Right: brick chimney of 1780.

openings in a wall called for classical treatment, but how was this to be correctly done when there were no models to look at from antiquity? The question was still being discussed in 1756, in which year Isaac Ware wrote in his book on architecture that

> those who have left rules and examples for other articles
> lived in hotter countries; and the chimney was not with
> them, as it is with us, a part of such essential importance
> that no common room, plain or elegant, could be
> constructed without it. Fancy is to stand in the place of rule
> and example in the construction of the chimney piece.

Somehow the sides of the fireplace had to represent classical columns, and lintels to represent their entablatures. Somehow it was done, and has never ceased to be done. Even where there are no actual columns beside a Georgian fireplace, the idea of them is felt in the proportions of the details, and in the way the sections correspond to base, shaft and capital.

Ware gave the most minute directions for making chimneypieces, and so did the writers of countless other manuals for builders. Anyone could learn about the recommended proportions, about the appropriate introduction and use of the various classical orders – in short, how to produce a fireplace with mouldings which had classical affiliations. There were a few takers for suggestions on how to flirt in a controlled manner with the Gothic and Chinese styles.

Simple fireplaces came to assume one of a few standard forms, each of them reflecting in some way the influence of the classical orders. Even bedrooms had fires now, though it is doubtful if they were used much except when the occupant was ill.

Semi-classical fireplaces – some had actual columns – had been produced before the eighteenth century: as early as 1624 Sir Henry Wotton had written on how to raise fair mantels in a classical manner, but examples are seen to be less-than-confident essays and for large houses only. A typical fireplace surround of the late seventeenth century, a type favoured by Wren, consisted of a plain S-bolection moulding, six to eight inches across, outlining the opening in oak panelling.

This fireplace with a plain moulding was superseded by the type with a shouldered architrave, and among variations introduced were inverted scrolls at the sides, and a keystone or tablet above the opening to break up the long line of the entablature. Perhaps the chimneypiece most characteristic of the main Georgian period was the sort whose pilasters, or uprights, merged into consoles under the cornice. As yet, a mantelshelf in the modern sense was not provided, though there are instances of a mantelshelf having been added later.

Except in great houses, the richly ornamented overmantel was

50 Queen Anne fireplace with a narrow shouldered architrave. This type was favoured for much of the Georgian period – often with unfortunate variations – and redeveloped by Robert Adam.

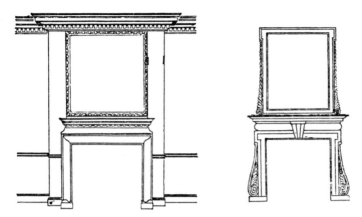

51 Early Georgian fireplaces with entablatures above. Left:
bolection moulding. Right: shouldered architrave with inverted
scrolls at the sides.

rarely built. A modestly enriched panel to receive a picture (or,
when the chimneypiece was of the shouldered kind, a large
mirror to match) generally sufficed; and even in minor houses the
chimneybreast over the fireplace might be distinguished by an
arrangement of three panels, a wide panel for a picture between
two narrow ones.

Single-storey chimneypieces following late eighteenth-
century designs by Robert Adam were in themselves satisfyingly
complete compositions; they were also boldly and obviously
classical in derivation. The mantelshelf was now quite wide.
Grand examples might have the female figure of Greek
architecture to support them. Among ordinary fireplaces, a
popular design had once more the shouldered surround which
originated in the seventeenth century; the now fashionable neo-
classical decoration would be applied to it. An important feature
of the Adam-style fireplaces was the central plaque. Where the
surrounds were to be of painted wood, ornament in low relief was
available ready-made; and the ease with which neo-classical
ornaments could be made with moulds brought elegant little
chimneypieces within the reach of all.

The use of wood was a late development: marble is the characteristic material for Georgian fireplaces and even the small ones would have a surround and hearthstone of marble. Occasionally the marble supplied was not quite what it seemed, to judge by Mrs Burton's quotations from correspondence in the 1730s between Henry Purefoy and a stone cutter of Bedford Row, London. Purefoy, who was having a simple fireplace renewed in Buckinghamshire, had ordered a hearth slab in purple marble, but when it arrived he noticed that it seemed 'cract in some places and as though it had bits of something put into it artificially'. The stone cutter assures him that all will be well, but in due course Purefoy writes to report that the marble 'blisters and rises up' and that a piece has broken off to reveal 'a coarse

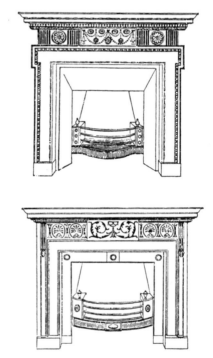

52 Mid-Georgian fireplaces in the Adam style fitted with grates. A typical feature of the surround is the central plaque on the frieze.

53 Late Georgian hob grates. Left: the popular duck's nest, presenting a double semi-circle. Right: a less common form shaped on each side to a double ogee. Front casings were embellished in high relief ready for being highly polished with black lead. Hob grates are commonly found to bear the name Carron: the Carron Foundry of Scotland was started in 1759.

stone like freestone'. Further, there are cracks into which he can thrust a pin.

At this period (late eighteenth century) the free-standing fire basket was superseded by the fixed grate, generally with bowed bars and often with a pierced apron. For bedrooms and lesser living rooms the hob grate made its appearance, a popular form for this being the double semi-circle, giving the duck's nest grate. When it was found that flues worked better when they were smaller, chimneybreasts were made to protrude scarcely more than the depth of the grate.

If free-standing stoves had been adopted, as on the Continent, rooms would have been warmer and less draughty, but these were never popular in England. A visible source of heat was what was wanted, and indeed the habit of sitting by an open fire led to the introduction of special or adapted pieces of furniture. There was, for example, the firescreen, ubiquitous in the eighteenth century in the form of a pole with sliding panels decorated with painting or needlework. There were firescreen desks at which the writer could sit with his face (and not his feet) shielded from the heat.

In the kitchen, wide homely fireplace openings were still needed to accommodate the machinery of cooking. Pots, frying pans and kettles swung from chains over the open fire and meat

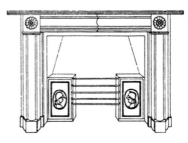

54 Regency fireplace. The better examples are of marble and give an effect which is refined and simple. The hobs shown above already suggest the kitchen range and the idea of heating water in one of them.

was roasted before it on spits. The oven would be built into the wall beside the fireplace, where it had to be heated separately.

The great fireplaces of the kitchens did not begin to be filled up with ranges of cast iron until towards the end of the century. The Rumford Stove, invented by Benjamin Thompson, was one of the first of the kitchen ranges and had a built-in oven and a boiler – with tap – for heating water. Ranges immediately made cooking easier but, using fuel voraciously, they were no more economical than the room-warming grates in their handsome Adam surrounds.

15

NON-CLASSICAL WORK

Followers of the architects' pattern books had the novel experience in the late eighteenth century of being invited to choose between ordering a Gothic or a classical house. Suddenly it seemed to be in order to have a house diametrically different from the kind which everyone all his life had supposed to be the only acceptable kind.

The Gothic way of building, especially for churches, abbeys and castles, had been out of fashion (though not forgotten) for 200 years, so that to see it in the Georgians' equivalent of catalogues, page after page of it, was even more curious than the experience in our own day of being offered new brass bedsteads in the ornamented Victorian style.

Attempts to revive for houses the features of Gothic church building had in fact been made from the beginning of the Georgian period, but it meant nothing to the general public that enthusiasts for 'the magnificence of our ancestors' had been accommodated, reluctantly, by Sir Christopher Wren and William Kent; that rich men sometimes found it piquant to erect small mediaeval buildings in their grounds (e.g. the ornamental cottage by a lake at Stourhead); that leisured clergymen loved to build Gothic summer houses in their gardens, with Early English features copied from the church: the Rev. William Stukeley of Stamford was preparing Gothic architectural drawings in the 1730s and built in the vicarage garden a Gothic Temple of Flora ('It suits the place'), in which his wife kept her pot plants.

The mediaeval Gothic system at its best had been structural, so that arches, piers and other supports, instead of being clothed, were themselves enriched to please the eye. Batty Langley, the publishing carpenter, was interested enough in stray revivals to publish in 1742 an exposition seeking to show that Gothic methods could be forced to conform at least partially with the disciplines of Rome, and that they might therefore be worth a try for domestic architecture. His *Gothic Architecture Improved by Rules and Proportions* made little more than a talking point; for so overwhelming was the draw of the clean-lined Palladian-Renaissance style that when revived Gothicism was encountered – in trifling buildings – it was dismissed as the work of the

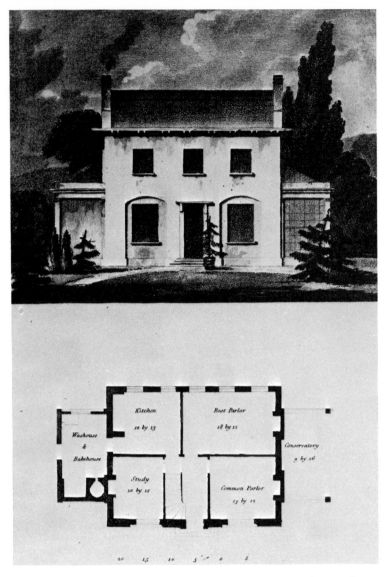

Kitchen
12 by 15

Best Parlor
18 by 12

Washouse
&
Bakehouse

Conservatory
9 by 16

Study
10 by 12

Common Parlor
13 by 12

20   15   10   5   0   5

55   Classical design described as 'a very comfortable residence for a family with a small independent fortune, or a retreat [in which] occasionally to relax from the bustle of business'. Note the recessed windows, typical of the period. From John Plaw, *Sketches for Country Houses, Villas and Rural Dwellings*, 1800.

eccentric or of romantic clergymen. A business man in Garrick and Coleman's play of 1766, *The Clandestine Marriage*, is made fun of for having at his country place a Gothic dairy and an octagonal gazebo.

For most of the period the Gothic taste was something exotic that was socially permitted (like the good joke of artificial mediaeval ruins in the garden) only in little additions to the outside or inside of classical houses. There are several examples of Gothic entrances, even one in Bath, allegedly designed by the great classical architect John Wood junior, and several examples of Gothic fireplaces. Gothic-looking pieces of furniture were sometimes thought to contrast creditably with their surroundings, and Thomas Chippendale, in his plates for *The Gentleman and Cabinet-maker's Director* gave prominence to designs with Gothic enrichment. William Whitehead, writing of Gothic forms in 1753 for the *World* observes that 'there is something, they say, congenial in them to our old Gothic constitution' and refers to beds, bookcases and couches that are 'copied from some parts or other of our old cathedrals'.

The eighteenth century saw, too, waves of Chinese taste. *Chinoiserie* was largely inspired by Sir William Chambers, architect of Somerset House, who had visited China and in 1753 published a book called *Designs of Chinese Buildings*. The first results of this were such that Whitehead was able to write expansively that in some houses the Chinese idea cropped up in 'chairs, tables, frames for looking glasses' and that 'even our most vulgar utensils are now reduced to this new fangled standard'; out of doors, he said, it had spread to the extent that 'every gate to a cow-yard is in Ts and Zs, and every hovel for the cows has bells hanging at its corners'. William Cowper wrote rather scathingly of a clergyman who 'enclosed his gooseberry bushes within a Chinese rail' and would not have approved of the Rev. William Cole's Chinese-Gothic garden temple at Bletchley in Buckinghamshire, its oak pillars and frieze of open lacework done under his directions by a carpenter who had never attempted such work before.

Horace Walpole's house, Strawberry Hill, on the Thames near

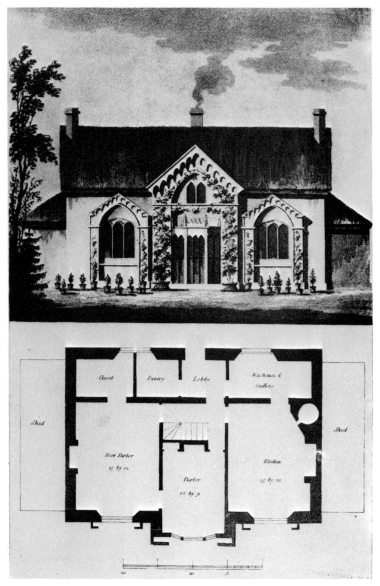

56 Gothic design described as 'a comfortable retreat from the bustle of town for the man of business or science'; it could be built of 'pisé, mud, rubble-stone or brick'. From John Plaw, *Sketches for Country Houses, Villas and Rural Dwellings*, 1800.

133

57 A mid-Georgian garden temple in the Chinese style at a house called Woodside near Windsor. From a drawing by Thomas Robins, the elder, 1750.

Twickenham, was prepared in the early 1750s and is one of the earliest and most notable examples of a whole house in the Gothic manner. It did not precipitate much imitation, but it was a great curiosity, drawing crowds of sightseers, and later when the Gothic revival was in force, it affected architectural thought, especially on the Gothic as an element in the Picturesque, because those who practised the cult of the Picturesque sought to create from scratch the accidentally pleasing effects often produced by a huddle of ancient buildings.

Strawberry Hill, when Walpole bought it in 1750, was an ordinary small Georgian house. Walpole proceeded over several years to obliterate the balanced elevations and encase everything in his own version of the mediaeval. He collected details and stuck them on as trophies. Nothing was symmetrical. Extensive additions included a round tower attached to an angle with no second tower to balance it. Sir John Summerson has generously written that the message of the house (attended to years later by people of discernment) was that 'a modern Gothic building should seek its authority not merely in the composition of this or that authority, but in the actual monuments of the Middle Ages'.

In the thirty years that followed the unveiling of Strawberry Hill, several factors or trends in Georgian society prepared the ground for the Gothic revival in house building. One of these was a fashion for reading novels, in particular romances with a mediaeval setting of the kind represented by *The Castle of Otranto*, by Horace Walpole himself (1765), and *The Old English Baron* by Clara Reeve (1777). Such books provided not so much stories in tune with mediaeval thought and feeling as stories appropriate to a setting of ruined abbeys, crumbling Gothic arches, ridges of wild mountains and groves of old oaks. Stirring natural scenery was so much admired that parties undertook coach outings to admire views held to be picturesque.

Another factor – it served to weaken the Palladian-Renaissance tradition – was acceptance of new classical styles, of which examples are the Adam version and revived ancient Greek. Why not break away altogether, it began to be asked, and build in a way that was both more British and more picturesque? The architects and others who turned out pattern books pressed the claims of a sort of house, commonly thatched, which had nothing to do with ancient Greece or Rome; and in a short time small Gothic houses began to appear all over the country, a striking characteristic being re-created mediaeval gables accompanied by barge-boards which were sometimes fretted.

House-builders vied with each other over the forming of Gothic features of every description, the craftsmen enthusiastically applying their skills to pointed arches, dripstones, battlements and window tracery. Having little knowledge of the origin of the Gothic system, they felt no restraint – in the

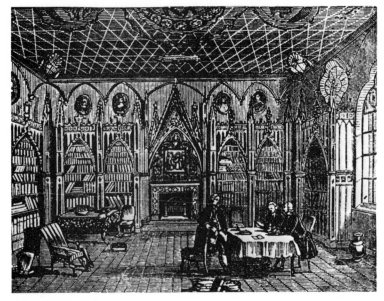

58 Mid-Georgian Gothic library at Strawberry Hill, Horace Walpole's house.

absence of masons – in carrying out designs in plaster or wood.

At the beginning of the nineteenth century the Gothic revival was fuelled further by Sir Walter Scott's Waverley novels, with their long descriptions of mediaeval scenes and buildings. Foundries met a demand for the look of leaded lights in mullioned windows by producing iron casements; these had glazing bars forming groups of hexagonal panes and ably resisted the wind.

The architect John Papworth held with many contemporaries that Gothic was the best and godliest style for a parsonage and in his book *Rural Residences*, 1818, wrote of one design that it was

intended for the residence of a clergyman, and to be erected in a situation where the scenery is both rural and romantic. The parts of this design are supposed to be selected from the church itself to which the vicarage-house belongs, and with which it should correctly assimilate, particularly if the

59 Regency Gothic house. From J. B. Papworth, *Rural Residences*, 1818.

60   Late Georgian Gothic porch (Sidmouth).

building be intended to be placed in its immediate
neighbourhood. The practice of designing the residence of a
clergyman with reference to the characteristics of the church
to which it belongs . . . is desirable, not only as relates to a
tasteful advantage, but as it becomes another and visible
link of connection between the church itself and the pastor
who is devoted to its duties; and also leads the spectator very
naturally from contemplating the dwelling, to regard the
pious character of its inhabitant.

A number of new Gothic parsonages had been built in the late
eighteenth century – the rectory at Charlton Mackrell, Somerset,
is an example – and classical ones had been given a Gothic skin.
The former vicarage of St Mary's, Newbury, Berkshire, built as a
classical red-brick house, was given a battlemented parapet and
its windows were made to rise to points beneath dripstones.

The Gothic parsonage is always associated with the reign of
Queen Victoria, so it is interesting to find it being produced well
before the beginning of her reign. Parsonages of the early Gothic
revival period have a lighthearted charm which is absent from

the sterner, spikier, dark red parsonages which were later to become so prevalent. Lighthearted pilfering of genuine Gothic work sometimes took place, according to Mr Anthony Bax: the former rectory at Wookey in Somerset sports an implanted oriel window and four spandrels of trefoil arcading with thirteenth-century sculptures taken, it is alleged, from Wells Cathedral.

Surviving work suggests that far more houses in fact continued to be built in a classical style than in the Gothic style, but the latter as the alternative was very noticeable. Louis Simond stayed in the Isle of Wight in 1811 and reported for French readers that Cowes was a pretty place with many gentlemen's houses near it.

> One of them is a Gothic castle, bran-new, stuck around with towers and battlements. Not far from it a poorer neighbour has erected his own Gothic thatched cottage. The Gothic style is considered here as national and they use it freely and as their own.

Some owners of small houses were amused to have them exhibit both Gothic and Greek features. Change for the sake of it now seemed important and, as with dress and hairstyles, so with their houses, people felt a need to be in what Jane Austen called 'a state of alteration, perhaps of improvement'.

16

THE VILLAS AND
THE END

The word villa took on a suburban connotation in England early in the eighteenth century – but only in the sense of a rich man's secondary residence. Towards the end of the century it meant, however, any little house that was above the ordinary with some architectural pretension, the genteel kind, boasting a scullery, which was referred to in Cowper's lines of 1782:

Suburban villas, highway side retreats,
That dread th' encroachment of our growing streets,
Tight boxes, neatly sashed. . . .

John Nash built several in the 1790s; they were very ornamental and formal. And during the period of the Napoleonic Wars villas for the well-to-do took up much of young architects' time because there was little other work for them. By 1800, indeed, this kind of building was in the forefront of architectural concern and shared with the Picturesque cottage, the *cottage ornée*, even the *ferme ornée*, the attention of the architects. David Laing, as busy as any with publishing books of designs with a view to taking commissions, begins his *Hints for Dwellings*, 1800, with an apology for adding 'another to the long catalogue of works already published' – but plenty more were to follow. 'Architecture, especially in its application to the conveniences of polished life', said Laing, 'is capable of an infinite variety of distributions and combinations, as well internal as external.'

The introduction in some of the pattern books seeks to show a difference between a *cottage ornée* and a small villa. In fact there was hardly any difference: a new type of house had arrived and

61　A Palladian villa of *c.* 1540 by Palladio. It is the Villa Godi at Lonedo, Italy, which may still be seen. Like many of the late Georgian villas of England, it has an elevated site. From Andrea Palladio, *Quattro Libri.*

all were similar in size and plan, and projecting according to taste, either urbanity or rusticity. The word cottage took on a secondary meaning for educated people and became short for *cottage ornée*, a building which might have a double coach house at the back. Jane Austen, writing in *Persuasion* of the marriage of a young squire, says that his village thereupon 'received the improvement of a farmhouse, elevated into a cottage, for his residence, and Uppercross Cottage, with its veranda, French windows, and other prettinesses, was quite as likely to catch the traveller's eye as the more consistent and considerable aspect and premises of the Great House about a quarter of a mile farther on'.

In the Regency period – that transitional period of Georgian building which was to change almost overnight around 1830 into the markedly different Victorian manner – nearly everyone wanted his house, however small, to catch not only the eye of travellers, as Jane Austen said, but also of anyone living in the neighbourhood.

It was not just that through affluence certain sections of the middle class were becoming pretentious and overdoing things: they didn't talk about it, but they half-feared a revolution in England on the lines of the recent successful revolution in France. On its face, Regency society seemed to be stratified in an amicable manner. There was a land-owning élite, a trading middle class and the rest who were poor; but the rest were getting poorer and – some noted – in actual numbers they represented over 90 per cent of the population. A Regency preoccupation with building villas on hilltops and ridges was partly inspired by a determination to throw off rain water (dampcourses had not been invented and Regency walls were thin), partly by a desire for a view and partly by ill-defined thoughts of revolution and uprisings: an elevated site could be felt to be an advantage, and where a house had battlements in the Gothic manner, these could be vaguely reassuring, however unsuitable for crouching behind with a gun.

John Byng, the indefatigable traveller about England, invented the term 'stareabout' for the new little houses which were being set at the tops of hills. In his accounts, published as

62   Regency villa. Curved bays were often carried two or more
storeys high. Note the front door set within a porch with a rounded
arch.

The Torrington Diaries, he refers twice to 'modern hill-top
stareabouts' and remarks that they were 'exposed to every
tempest and distant from every comfort'. Louis Simond also
commented on the new airy sites for 'gentlemen's houses', while
Jane Austen devoted several pages of *Sanditon* to making fun of
them.

In this novel she writes of Mr Parker deserting his house in a
sheltered dip – it was well fenced and planted, and had orchards
and meadows – in favour of a new house draughtily sited on the
brow of a hill. Charlotte, a girl being brought by Mr Parker for a
visit, says the wrong thing as they pass the former, sheltered
house. 'And whose very snug-looking place is this?' 'Ah', says Mr
Parker with determined satisfaction. 'This is my old house', and
he explains that he has given it up to a tenant called Hillier. 'Our
ancestors, you know,' he tells Charlotte, 'always built in a hole.'

But Mrs Parker cannot help remarking on how comfortable it
was and looks at it 'through the back window of the carriage with
the fondness of regret'. She remarks: 'It was a nice place for the
children to run about in. So shady in summer. . . . The Hilliers
did not seem to feel the storms last winter at all. I remember

seeing Mrs Hillier after one of those dreadful nights, when we had been literally rocked in our bed, and she did not seem at all aware of the wind being anything more than common.' But Mr Parker is ready with his rejoinder. 'Yes, yes – that's likely enough. *We* have all the grandeur of the storm, because the wind, meeting with nothing to oppose or confine it around our house, simply rages and passes on – while down in the gutter nothing is known of the state of the air, below the tops of the trees.'

As they reach the top of the downs Charlotte notes 'with the calmness of amused curiosity' little houses called Prospect House and Bellevue Cottage. The Parkers' residence is especially high up, 'a light elegant building standing in a small lawn with a very young plantation round it'. Here Jane Austen has Mr Parker explaining that shade will soon be provided on the hill by the growth of his plantations, already 'a general astonishment', and she must surely have smiled over Mr Parker's next remark: 'In the mean while we have the canvas awning, which gives us the most complete comfort within doors.' Shown into her room, Charlotte 'found amusement in standing at her ample Venetian window, and looking over the miscellaneous foreground of unfinished buildings, waving linen. . . .'

Comments on the snobbish state of mind of smart-villa owners are offered by William Howitt, writing at the end of the Regency period in *Rural Life in England*:

Every man lives now-a-day for public observation. He builds his house and organizes his establishment so as to strike public opinion as much as possible . . . nothing can be more lamentable, and were it not lamentable, nothing could be more ludicrous, than the state of rivalry, heart-burning jealousy, personal mortification, or personal pride, from mere accidents of condition or favour. The titled have a fixed rank, and are comparatively at their ease, but in the great mass of those who have wealth, more or less, without title, what a mighty and eating sore is the struggle for distinction . . . The lower you descend in the social scale, the more exacting becomes the spirit of exclusiveness. The

63 Late Regency Greek Doric portico.

professionals look down on the trades; the trades on one another. Everywhere the same uneasy spirit shows itself.

In Howitt's opinion, slights, dead cuts and things of that sort with their consequent heart-burnings 'pressed the charm of existence out of the hearts of thousands and made the country often a purgatory where it might have been a paradise'.

For some who built near towns private enterprise and progress made the country, so far as they were concerned, no longer rural. Many a man who, after the Battle of Waterloo, had built himself a stylish villa on a dusty road leading out of town found that he was surrounded on every side by other equally stylish villas – Greek, French, Italian, Gothic; each with an ample garden.

This clearly was suburban development. The tighter development along main roads leading from the middle of an old town towards its outskirts provides today a revealing sequence of domestic building. At the start of the road the houses may be modernized mediaeval, then Tudor or Georgian-fronted Tudor, then Georgian with perhaps a late-Georgian terrace, then Regency, then Victorian in the form of gaunt Italianate semis or of Gothic detached residences whose occupants were for a time 'in

64 Regency recessed doorcase based on the Greek Doric order.

the country'. Finally there may come a succession of separate houses and semis plainly dating from that part of the twentieth century when ribbon development was still permitted.

Builders and architects of the Georgian Renaissance period took seriously, as has been said earlier, the fun of harmless deception. So did those of the Regency. Nash developed the device whereby two or three small houses were clapped together in such a way that they give, collectively, the appearance of one substantial villa. In Regent's Park, after practising it elsewhere, he did this in a way which is not appreciated without investigation; the houses of York Terrace, as Sir John Summerson has pointed out, comprise not only the two terraces proper (east and west), but also several villas which in turn are split into two or more separate houses. In the Park villages, the houses dating from 1824 are all in pairs, each pair giving the appearance outside of one villa – in the Gothic, Tudor, Italian, French or Greek style.

Disguising two small houses to seem one amounts to nothing

146

more than building semi-detached houses and giving them a unifying feature to distract the eye – such a feature as a pediment, a gable, a fake central window or just an inscribed panel. The semi was not in itself a novelty. There is an example in Hampstead, 22 and 24 Rosslyn Hill, dated 1702. As farm workers' accommodation, semis had been found friendly to live in since the middle of the eighteenth century – and economical to build because only one central chimney stack was needed. The semi, however, began its socially successful career only after the introduction of the unified villa exterior. Once this treatment was established nothing could stop the word villa descending lower and even being applied to each semi-detached house in a pair. This was happening freely in the 1870s, and at suitable dates Jubilee Villas were erected by the thousand.

London led the way in suburban villa-building but, towards the end of the Regency, architects, squeezed out by speculative builders, found more scope for their skills in the provinces. Thus towns like Bath, Clifton, Worthing and Brighton show more interesting examples than St John's Wood, Clapham and Brixton of this last phase of Renaissance house-building, whether part-Palladian or part-Adam.

The final flourish of the Georgian building period as a whole was the lavish use of stucco, readily covering all and taking stylistic motifs. Today the white or colour-washed stucco on Regency houses – where the effort is made to maintain it – gives them a well-mannered look, and is especially associated with the domestic architecture of the first twenty-five years of the nineteenth century.

In towns by the sea, many of the houses of this period are now happily converted into hotels and holiday apartments: they can be seen all along the coast as far west as Weymouth. It has been recognized that much of the charm of Regency buildings lies in well-bred frivolity, and owners have responded by painting the stucco blue or pink. Modern colour-fast paints have helped to reveal the appropriateness of the buildings to their seaside setting.

THE SMALL REGENCY HOUSE (*c.* 1800–30), SOME CHARACTERISTICS

The Greek revival influence is often seen in a porch sporting the Greek Doric or Ionic order. Greek elevations are low with a dwarfed attic storey, a low-pitched pediment and windows with very thin glazing bars, the windows being set in shallow recesses in the wall. The cornice below the parapet is likely to show the echinus moulding illustrated on page 149 (a sure sign of Greek revival influence).

Houses of the Regency unaffected by revival influence – except the popular, round-arched recess for the front door – are nearly always marked by a very low-pitched, double-span roof with wide projecting eaves and modillions (projecting supports) in pairs. Where such houses are unstuccoed, in and around London, many are faced with refined yellow-grey brick, though sides and back may show coarser brick.

The sash windows have their boxes containing the counter-weights largely concealed in the brickwork. To avoid having only a paltry strip of these boxes visible, it became the fashion to

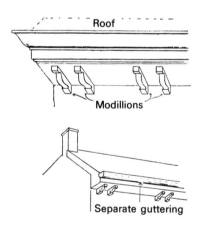

65   Details of shallow Regency roofs on houses unaffected by revival influence. Wide projecting eaves with modillions in twos or threes are usual.

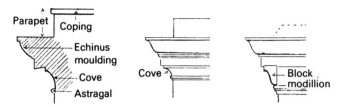

66 Regency external cornices.

increase the width of the window frame in order to show four or five inches of this. Carefully shaped external pelmets to windows and ironwork grilles to the sills of upper windows are both features seen on ordinary Regency houses. Where a front door is not recessed it has pilasters – plain, fluted or reeded – which often carry a simple device on the frieze such as a patera or a shape based on the square of a rectangle.

There are many examples of Regency houses with stuccoed fronts so simple that they are broken only by the slight semi-circular or segmental arched recesses in which windows are set. In the fashionable areas of important towns, the architecture of the Regency house in general continued the Georgian tradition in its respect for rules of proportion and dignity in design; the Adam manner, too, is evident in the restrained embellishment of exteriors and in the subordination of an individual house to the conception of the group.

Another distinguishing feature of the small Regency house is the curved bay window, possibly repeating itself through four storeys, and the semi-hexagonal bay. A large curved central bay may be found at the back of a house overlooking the garden.

Regency Gothic houses have all or most of the following: a battlemented parapet; pointed casement windows with tracery in the heads; drip moulds over the windows; a porch with clusters of narrow engaged shafts; a pointed front-door case with either half-clusters of narrow shafts or reeding which continues up to form an arch; windows associated with balconies, hooded or unhooded.

Broadly speaking, all Regency houses are either classical or Gothic. The Battle of the Two Styles was beginning, and some

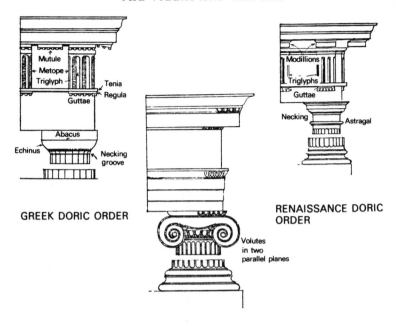

GREEK DORIC ORDER

RENAISSANCE DORIC ORDER

GREEK IONIC ORDER

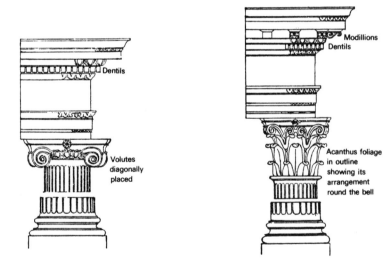

RENAISSANCE IONIC ORDER

RENAISSANCE CORINTHIAN ORDER

architects played safe by introducing both at once. But the phrase 'dainty Regency' covers all, and there was every promise in the 1820s that that ever more pleasing small houses would follow. Instead a reaction set in; architects researched every aspect of architectural history, and what in fact followed was a welter of ill-digested Styles of Architecture. To realize the abruptness of the change, it is only necessary to compare pattern books of the late 1820s with J. C. Loudon's *Encyclopaedia of Cottage, Farm and Villa Architecture* of 1833, and to note in his hundreds of examples of small houses how the Georgian manner had been replaced by heavy Italianate, a new stern Gothic, old English, Swiss and numerous styles associated with the past, even 'Indian Gothic' – all now easily recognized as simply Victorian.

67   The classical orders. Behind the details of Georgian domestic architecture there was a strong appreciation of the Roman, the Renaissance and, later, the Greek orders of architecture, these orders being certain ways of treating columns and their entablatures.

A column is a pillar of circular section, especially one which widens out at the foot to form a base and at the top to form a capital. An entablature is a lintel resting on the columns, and it is normally divided into three horizontal parts. These, from the bottom, are architrave, frieze and cornice. The cornice consists of a projecting upper part and a recessed under part known as a bed mould. The term architrave means too, of course, the frame of a doorway or window opening.

17

ARCHIVAL RECORDS

It is sometimes possible for those concerned with a particular small Georgian house to learn about its early history, or the history of its locality, in the repositories of county, parish or diocese, or in a public library. Old documents are still being found concealed in houses, bundled away under floors or in roof spaces, and householders are recommended to shine a torch when boards are lifted for re-wiring work. Any county archives department can give news of pleasing finds of this sort which have been duly reported to them.

A friend, Hugh Malet, in 1976 had to re-wire a Georgian village-house he had just bought beside a canal at Bartington in Cheshire, and he tells me that his electrician came upon 'a substantial bundle of old papers and parchment sheets just above the ceiling of the second floor landing': these included canal freight bills made out for the Duke of Bridgewater and revealed that a flourishing trade in farm produce had been carried on from the house in the early eighteenth century.

The Historical Manuscripts Commission in Chancery Lane, London, has from time to time proved a useful starting point for searchers, especially if the house in question is a manor house or was formerly part of a landed estate known as a manor. The commission keeps a manorial documents register, arranged alphabetically by parishes, of the addresses at which old administrative papers may be consulted. Their collections of papers – of all kinds – are added to at the rate of about 1,000 a year. Serious students may profit too, by consulting John Harvey's *Sources of the History of Houses* which was published in 1974 by the British Records Association.

The documents likely to provide the most satisfactory information include surveys of private estates, and valuations and probate inventories made out following the death of occupants. Local newspapers are a possible source; for, where a freehold is known to have changed hands at certain times, a diligent search of the files of appropriately dated journals could yield a now-curious description prepared as a property advertisement. Recommendations like 'malt kiln at the back to be converted to offices' have an almost modern look. Here is an advertisement in

153

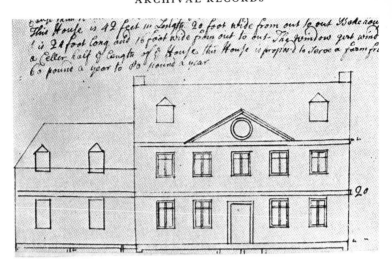

68 Design for a farmhouse, prepared by a building craftsman, in the archives of Essex County Council, *c.* 1750. The desire for a classical façade had spread down the social scale.

the *Kentish Gazette* of 9 July 1768, for a modest-sized house at Margate to be sold to the highest bidder:

> All that new-built Brick Dwelling House. . . . Containing 4 rooms on a floor, a turret on the top of the House and very good cellars; with a very good Reservoir for Rain-water, a Pump from a fine spring, Kitchen and Pleasure Gardens, Coachhouse, Stable and 2 acres of Pasture Land inclosed. . . . Particulars from Mr Fagg, Attorney of Ramsgate.

To save wear and tear of early newspapers, it has sometimes been arranged that the public can look at them by means of the microfilm system.

For information about old vicarages and rectories, there are the glebe terriers, these being reports about their accommodation which incumbents had to send from time to time to the diocesan authorities. Most documents are more likely to describe houses that already exist than the construction of new ones.

Estate maps of farms are sometimes found to be embellished with little drawings of the farmhouse which, though not architecturally accurate, show the approximate size of a house at the time the map was made, how many chimney stacks it had, where the front door used to be, if there was a pond, the siting of an approach lane. The drawings on maps of small houses are the nearest equivalent to the contemporary paintings and engravings made of the great Georgian houses. For these showpieces, correspondence with craftsmen has probably been preserved, but correspondence to do with the small houses is rare: formal contracts and receipts may never have been prepared.

A probate inventory may occasionally be turned up which gives the occupant of an old house a picture of how his rooms were once furnished. If dated around 1700, it might read in part:

	£	s	d
In ye Hall			
Item one Table 6 Stooles 4 Chaires			
one little Table	1	6	8
In ye best Parler			
One Table and one Carpit			
Six Chaires 2 Stooles and one			
Hand Iron	5	0	0
In ye Chamber			
One Bedstead with Bedinge			
thereto belonging	7	0	0
One little Table and other			
things there	1	10	0

Examples of the kind of information stored in the archives of one architecturally-conscious county, Kent, will serve to illustrate what might be found in most parts of Britain. This county, which has published a useful booklet about its collection, holds numerous surveys of the estates of landowning families and of public bodies. They often give details of the condition of farmhouses and manor houses with suggestions for alteration: they also show that in Kent, at least, a manor house need be no grander than a farmhouse, being so called because it was the residence of a rent-collecting tenant farmer or bailiff. The Records Office at Maidstone holds accounts of building work completed; though in many cases, where the tenant and not the landlord was responsible for repairs, these are only entries to the effect that so much was charged by Smith the carpenter. Tradesmen's bills seldom give more than the briefest details of what they did, with the cost of labour and materials.

Estimates tend to be more informative, even if it is not possible to find out if the work was ever carried out in the form advised. But estimates, especially when accompanied by plans, can be of interest as evidence of the sort of modernization that was going on at a particular time to suit new needs and architectural fashions. There emerge again and again estimates for enlarging an old house in brickwork to form a square, with single-span roofs side by side, estimates for dividing a house to form two dwellings for workers and their families. It becomes clear, too, that throughout the eighteenth century plenty of houses continued to be framed in oak, covered over, in a way that had hardly varied for centuries.

The estate maps still exist which were ordered by Sir Edward Filmer. He succeeded to the East Sutton Park Estate in 1720 and ran it for thirty years, clearly concerning himself closely with improvements to farmhouses. The plans show experiments with wings for enlarging houses, and ingenious ways of making three cottages out of one old farmhouse. They also show original plans and how the use of rooms had changed since the sixteenth and seventeenth centuries. The hall, or main living room, was now called the kitchen, and the small parlour – where people had often slept – had become a wash-house or a brew-house. (This room was later to become the withdrawing room and then just the drawing room.) There are illustrations of proposals to put on classical façades.

The archives hold a letter from a tenant farmer of Selling complaining strongly about the condition of his house, a letter which almost at once led to a building craftsman being asked to replace the house. The farmer wrote as follows:

Gentlemen,
Sirs, I am tenant of Stone Stile Farm in the parish of
Selling. Beg you will take it in consideration in respect to the
house as it is in such a state as impossible to leve in it in the

present state with my famely. Think it may be repard with puteng new wall around it, as the house is bursting in two parts, or a new one as you have got the plan of in your pocessoon. Gentelmen as you think most proper and will oblige yours to command.

Thomas Berry

The builder proposed a simple, square, brick farmhouse with the roof consisting of two spans joined and an outside staircase for the servants' attic bedrooms. Here is his letter:

Sir,
The enclose'd plans, using all the old materials taken down, which are sound and good, with one celler under the parlour and one garret in the roof; the two principal floors 7 feet high when finish'd, the external walls $1\frac{1}{2}$ bricks thick – 4 inch bricknog'd and render'd partitions on the ground floor and 3 inch ditto lath and plaster'd and render'd in bedchamber floor; the garrets plaster'd and ceil'd 6 ft. 6 in. high; the roof cover'd with plain tiles; the garret and bedchambers floor'd with inch white deal; the parlour floor'd with inch yellow deal and the offices and cellar paved with brick; two and three light window frames glaz'd with green glass in lead and inch ledg'd doors and iron latches to all the rooms; the whole executed in a workmanlike manner exclusive of painting will cost one hundred ninety six pounds, £196.
   I am Sir, with the greatest respect, your most obliged obedient servant.

John Worthy

Current and former houses of the clergy, which in Georgian times were usually no bigger than the neighbouring houses of farmers and villagers, tend to be well documented in the records of the dioceses, the terrier reports giving the building materials of the house (including its flooring) the general state of repair, the names of the rooms and the siting of the fireplaces.

   The glebe terriers of the Rochester diocese (these are housed in

157

the Kent Archives department) reveal mediaeval houses quite unaltered in the eighteenth century, mediaeval houses Georgianized, typical sixteenth and seventeenth century houses of the long, timbered type and Georgian brick houses large and small.

The vicarage at Hadlow had clearly changed out of recognition by the mid-eighteenth century. The terrier of 1662, signed by the vicar and his churchwarden, reveals a hall house. There is

> an hall without any ceiling, being open to the top, two lower chambers within the hall, over which one upper chamber, one kitchen open also to the top, one parlour with an upper chamber over it, and 'tis all covered with thatch and the house stands in about one acre of gleabe land.

The description of the house sent a hundred years later, in 1761, reads as follows:

> This house is built with bricks and tiled and consisteth of a kitchen on the left hand and a parlour on the right with two closets to the same. Facing the kitchen door is a pantry and cellar; on the west side of this house is an outlet which serves for brewhouse and vault on the right hand. On the left hand of the stairs a small chamber and parlour chamber. On the right hand are two chambers with two closets, with two garrets. . . .

In some cases the evidence of glebe terriers about clergymen's houses can be supplemented by information from the probate inventory of an incumbent. Thomas Brewer died at Nettlestead Rectory in 1714. He was thirty-three and unmarried. The house was better furnished than that of many clergymen, the parlour having tapestry hangings and eight cane chairs (two with arms) which were grouped round an oval table. In the hall there were two more oval tables, a clock and fifteen maps on the walls. The best bedroom had curtains at the window. The closet was used as a study and contained an escritoire and a collection of books worth £20. It also contained articles emphasising the fact that the clergy were still working farmers: along with pots and pans and pewter plates, the rector had in his study husbandry tools, a corn fan, three sieves, a ladder and two hop bins, a parcel of hay and a stock of hop poles.

The rectory at Foots Cray is found to have been, throughout the Georgian period, a cottage measuring twenty feet by twelve; successive rectors made formal complaints about its smallness, but it was not until 1862 that money was obtained from Queen Anne's Bounty on mortgage for a rebuilding. In a letter of *c.* 1825, probably to one of the governors of Queen Anne's Bounty, a rector begins as follows (soon putting aside his attempt at punctuation):

My Lord,
When I assure you that the favour of your Lordship's opinion and advice may prove of essential benefit to the living of which I am the incumbent, I do not doubt that you will readily excuse my troubling you with the following particulars, respecting a proposed measure by which a more commodious residence may be obtained on terms advantageous to the living.

The present glebe house is an ancient and mean structure unfit for the residence of an incumbent with a family. Formerly it was let to persons of inferior condition at a very low rent but about twenty years since some repairs being made and a small kitchen added, the curate was required to reside and I did myself live there seven years but was ultimately obliged to remove to a more convenient residence and since my succession to the living as I could not with any regard to the comfort of my family return to the parsonage I obtained your Lordship's licence to occupy another house for the superior accommodations of which a greater rent is required than I can well afford to pay. . . .

The rectory at Ash-next-Ridley was stated in 1739 to be in so ruinous a condition, with several walls shored, that repairs to it would be dangerous. The plan and elevation for a new rectory, which are preserved in the archives, show a typical square, small Georgian house, a building very different from the long, narrow,

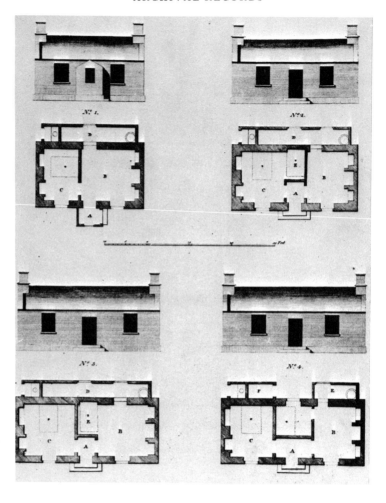

69   Small classical cottages. From John Wood junior, *Series of Plans for Cottages or Habitations of the Labourer*, 1781.

wood-framed houses of previous centuries: the drawings were executed in local flint with brick quoins, and the house is still in existence. The Bishop of Rochester was among those who had signed their name to an expression of opinion that 'succeeding rectors will receive manifest benefit by the building of an house according to the plan now laid before us'.

While a search for early references to small Georgian houses – even farmhouses and parsonages – may lead to nothing of interest, finding out history to do with a simple cottage is usually impossible. In the title deeds of farmholdings, cottages barely get a mention. In any case, hardly any existed before the middle of the eighteenth century – that is, cottages in the true sense of small dwellings erected by someone skilled at building for labourers.

18

THE GEORGIAN TRADITION REVIVED

As small Georgian houses gradually get knocked down, so they are more than replaced in numbers by new small houses sold as Georgian-style, a label known by all speculative builders to be good for sales. But the replacement seldom happens in the right places, showing itself in private housing estates on the edges of towns and in disjointed clusters at the seaside. As for the advertised style, it will be seen that the builders have merely played with the Georgian language and made it barely recognizable by getting the grammar all wrong. Look at front doors, proportions of windows, setting of roofs – to mention just three parts which cost no less to do incorrectly. With exceptions, the few satisfactory neo-Georgian houses built in the present century are fairly large ones designed to order by bespoke architects.

'Can we say that the classical tradition is completely lost, or does it only await the invigorating influence of new thought to produce new growth?' The question has often been expressed in the 1970s, but I am quoting from a book of 1905, *English Domestic Architecture in the Seventeenth and Eighteenth Centuries* by Horace Field and Michael Bunney. The authors go on to ask: 'Where can there be found a style which more directly answers modern requirements?' and they explain how the classical style 'suffers less than any other from the use of modern building aids'.

The attempts by the Modern Movement since 1905 to establish almost new kinds of house have made the comments of Field and Bunney especially applicable today, for it cannot be said, either that most modernist houses are standing the test of time, or that there has been a noticeable return to tradition more successful than half-hearted neo-, or Post Office, classicism. More people than ever may be asking why we cannot have again houses as obviously fit for their purpose and pleasing to the eye as the small ones of the late eighteenth century – the sort of house which Britain's best architects live in themselves. In fact, a few such houses have recently been ordered and inexpensively built. A change in taste seems imminent. London's planners have abruptly ditched the high rise block and gone back to stipulating terrace houses. Here and there the classical language of

70   A North London Georgian house modernized in 1930s style.

architecture is making sense again.

The phrase 'classical language of architecture', as applied to new building, was much used by Raymond Erith (1904–73), the most undeviating classical architect so far known by the twentieth century: he was responsible for a new entrance and cottages for Royal Lodge, Windsor (bombed in 1940), for the restoration of numbers 10, 11 and 12 Downing Street between 1958 and 1963 and for village-street houses of such classical simplicity that they are not at once distinguished from neighbours 250 years old.

An exhibition of pictures of Erith's work was held at the Royal Academy in 1976, where a succinct catalogue on sale had articles of praise by Sir Hugh Casson, Lucy Archer and Quinlan Terry. Drawing attention to the exhibition in *Country Life*, John Cornforth wrote that during recent years Erith's self-effacing designs 'no longer aroused hatred in planning officers brain-washed by the Modern Movement'.

Erith had been certain all his working life that classical architecture could be purified and re-stated; his small houses, detached and terrace, have as little to do with the popular conception of neo-Georgianism as with the Modern Movement. His terrace houses – for example the nine in Canonbury Place, London, N1, and three in Aubrey Walk, London, W 8 – appear at first, in their yellow London stock brick, to be exact copies of neighbouring houses, but inside there is a good deal of skilled adjustment for the sake of comfort and minor planning regulations. Where street houses had to face a noisy thorough-fare, Erith considered such problems as drastically reducing the number of front windows, while abiding by the regulations.

All his buildings show his confidence in classicism as a living tradition, also that he was an architect without pomposity. Some buildings show a sense of humour: for example, the Tempietto in Gibson Square, London N 1, which disguises a ventilation shaft for the Victoria Line.

One of the skills, other than those of draughtsmanship and knowledge of construction, which Erith expected from assistants was intelligent use of source books; Palladio's *Quattro Libri* and

71　The Georgian manner revived. A house, known as The Folly, completed by Raymond Erith in 1964 in Gately Park, Herefordshire. It shows how the eighteenth-century classical language can be used for an original design today.

the 1825 Paris edition of *Palladio's Works* were constantly in use. He did not advise students to go straight back to the orders of architecture, but rather 'to accept tradition in principle and certainly to stop avoiding traditional forms and methods', to 'accept the broad stream of tradition as a whole and then enlarge and expand it'.

As a member of the Royal Fine Art Commission between 1960 and 1963, Erith was involved in efforts to protect threatened buildings. These could not be always successful and he wrote to a friend in 1971: 'My hatred of the destruction of beauty begins to eat into my love of it, so that I find myself becoming a husk like the husks modernists make of Georgian terraces.' Told once that he had kept the lamp of classicism alight, he replied: 'Not alight, but smouldering.' He wrote in another letter of 1971: 'All my life I have been waiting for the revival of architecture. I do not think it *will* happen, but if the right idea could be put out at the right time, I think it could happen.' Meanwhile Erith's pupil who became his partner, Quinlan Terry, continues to build small houses in the classical language of the eighteenth century. Meanwhile, too, the Georgian Group and the numerous amenity societies of Britain exert themselves to awaken further public interest in the old Georgian buildings, and to save good ones, whatever their size, from wanton destruction and disfigurement.

BIBLIOGRAPHY

Ackerman, J. S., *Palladio*, Penguin, 1966.

Adam, R., *Works in Architecture*, 1773.

Adamson, G., *Machines at Home*, Lutterworth, 1969.

Askwith, B., *The Lytteltons*, Chatto & Windus, 1975.

Barley, M. W., *The English Farmhouse and Cottage*, Routledge & Kegan Paul, 1961.

Barley, M., *The House and Home*, Studio Vista, 1963.

Bax, B. Anthony, *The English Parsonage*, John Murray, 1964.

Bowen, E., *Chapters of an Autobiography*, Allen Lane, 1975.

Braun, H., *The Story of English Architecture*, Faber & Faber, 1954.

Braun, H., *Old English Houses*, Faber & Faber, 1964.

Brown, A., *Colchester in the Eighteenth Century*, A. F. J. Brown, 172 Lexden Road, Colchester, Essex.

Burton, E., *The Georgians at Home*, Longman, 1967.

Byng, J., journals of the 1790s edited by C. B. and F. Andrews as *The Torrington Diaries*, Eyre & Spottiswoode, 1954.

Chalkin, C. W., *The Provincial Towns of England*, Arnold, 1974.

Clifton-Taylor, A., *The Pattern of English Building*, Faber & Faber, 1972.

Cobbett, W., *Rural Rides*, 1830.

Cornforth, J., 'A Struggle for the Classic', *Country Life*, 7 October 1976.

Cruikshank, D., *London: the Art of Georgian Building*, Architectural Press, 1975.

Defoe, D., *Tour through the Island of Great Britain*, 1724–7.

de la Rochefoucauld, F., *Mélanges sur l'Angleterre, c.* 1784.

Downing, A. J., *The Architecture of Country Houses*, 1850, reissued by Dover Publications, 1969.

Fastnedge, R., *English Furniture Styles*, Penguin, 1955.

Field, H., and Bunney, M., *English Domestic Architecture in the Seventeenth and Eighteenth Centuries*, Bell, 1905.

Fiennes, C., journals of the earliest years of the eighteenth century edited by C. Morris as *The Journeys of Celia Fiennes*, Cresset Press, 1947.

Fletcher, V., *Chimney Pots and Stacks*, Centaur, 1968.

Forrester., H., *The Smaller Queen Anne and Georgian House*, Tindal Press, 1964.

Foskett, D., 'Georgian Domesticity in the North', *Country Life* 27 November 1975 and other articles in that journal during 1975.

Gardiner, S., *Evolution of the House*, Constable, 1975.

George, M. Dorothy, *England in Johnson's Day*, Methuen, 1928.

George, M. Dorothy, *England in Transition*, Penguin, 1953.

George, M. Dorothy, *Hogarth to Cruikshank: Social Change in Graphic Satire*, Lane, 1967.

Gloag, J., *A Short History of Furniture*, Allen, 1952.

Gloag, J., *Georgian Grace*, Black, 1956.

Harvey, J., *Sources of the History of Houses*, British Records Association, 1974.

Hellyer, S. S., *Plumbing*, 1873.

Henderson, A., *The Family House in England*, Phoenix, 1964.

Holme, T., *Chelsea*, Hamish Hamilton, 1972.

Howitt, W., *Rural Life in England*, 1838.

Innocent, C. F., *The Development of English Building Construction*, 1916.

Jenkins, S., *Landlords to London*, Constable, 1975.

Johnson, S., *Journey to the Western Isles of Scotland*, 1775.

Jones, S., *Old Houses in Holland*, 1908.

Kelly, A., *The Book of English Fireplaces*, Country Life, 1968.

Kent, N., *Hints to Gentlemen of Landed Property*, 1775.

Laing, D., *Hints for Dwellings*, 1801.

Langley, Batty, *The City and Country Workman's Treasury of Design*, 1741.

Le Blanc, J. B., *Letters on the English and French Nations*, translated 1747.

Loudon, J. C., *Encyclopaedia of Cottage, Farm and Villa Architecture*, 1833.

Lucas, Dr, *An Essay on Waters*, 1756.

Malton, J., *Designs for Villas*, 1802.

Mayhew, H., *London Labour and the London Poor*, 1851.

Moxon, J., *Mechanick Exercises*, 1678.

Osborne, A., *English Domestic Architecture*, Country Life, 1954.

Palmer, R., *The Water Closet*, David & Charles, 1973.

Palmer Cook, F., *Talk to Me of Windows*, Allen, 1971.

Papworth, J., *Rural Residences*, 1818.

Penoyre, J., and Ryan M., *The Observer's Book of Architecture*, Warne, *c.* 1955.

Pepys, S., diaries of 1660 to 1669 as edited by O. F. Morshead as *Everybody's Pepys*, Bell, 1926.

Pilcher, D., *The Regency Style*, Batsford, 1947.

Plaw, J., *Sketches for Country Houses, Villas and Rural Dwellings*, 1800.

Plumb, J. H., *England in the Eighteenth Century*, Penguin, 1950.

Ramsey, S., and Hervey, J., *Small Georgian Houses and their Details*, Architectural Press, 1972.

Seymour, J., *Companion Guide to East Anglia*, Collins, 1970.

Simond, L., journals of 1810–11 edited by Christopher Hibbert as *Journal of a Tour*, Maxwell, 1968.

Sterne, L., *Tristram Shandy*, 1767.

Summerson, J., *Architecture in Britain 1530 to 1830*, Penguin, 1953.

Summerson, J., *Georgian London*, Penguin, 1962.

Swift, J., *Directions to Servants*, 1731, published 1745.

Unstead, R., *The Rise of Great Britain 1688–1837*, Black, 1973.

Waistell, C., *Designs for Agricultural Buildings*, 1827.

Ware, I., *The Complete Body of Architecture*, 1756.

Williams-Ellis, C., *Building in Cob, Pisé and Stabilized Earth*, 1947.

Wood, J., senior, *Essay Towards a Description of Bath*, 1749.

Wood, J., junior, *Series of Plans for Cottages or Habitations of the Labourer*, 1781.

Woodforde, James, late eighteenth-century diary edited by John Beresford as *The Diary of a Country Parson*, Oxford, 1931.

Woodforde, John, *The Truth about Cottages*, Routledge & Kegan Paul, 1969.

Wright, L., *Clean and Decent*, Routledge & Kegan Paul, 1960.

INDEX

Acts: Building, 16, 31; Enclosure, 65, 69; London, 46; Rates, 109; Tithe, 84; Window, 117–18
Adam, Robert, 22–4, 36, 38, 149
Adamson, Gareth, 94
Adelphi buildings, 22, 36
advowson, 78
America, country houses, 73–5
Architecture, The Complete Body of, 107
Architecture of Country Houses, The, 73
architrave, 124–5, 151
archives, 153–61
Aris's Birmingham Gazette, 27
Ash-next-Ridley rectory, 159, 161
Askwith, Betty, 4
attic, dormered, 15, 17, 115
Attle, Parson, 80
Aubrey Walk, 165
Austen, Jane, 139, 142–3

Bailey, M. W., 67
balconies, 22, 149
balusters, 4, 21, 42, 50
bankruptcy, builders', 36
Barbon, Nicholas, 42
Barnsley, 114
Bartholomew Street, 26
Bath, 34, 72, 91, 99, 119, 132, 147
Bath, Essay Towards a Description, 88

bathroom, 108–9
Bax, B. Anthony, 84, 105, 139
Beccles, 36
bed mould, 14, 151
Bedford, Duchess of, 35
Bedford, Duke of, 37
Bedford Row, 44
Bedford Square, 35, 57
Bedfordshire, 10
bedroom, 99–103, 124
beer, 108
Bennison, Appleton, 27
Berkshire, 82, 138
Birmingham, 26–7, 37, 62
Bletchley, 118, 132
Blomefield, Rev. Francis, 82
Bloomsbury, 37
bolection moulding, 124–5
bonfires, mortar drying, 62
boom, housing, 34
Boswell, James, 105
Bow Street Runners, 54
Bradshaw, Rev. Robert, 80
Bretby Park, 114
Breton, Rev. Robert, 79
Brewer, Thomas, 158
brick: colour, 20, 59; digging for, 42; Flemish bond, 8, 44, 61, 63; laying, 44, 60–3; mathematical

tiles, 8; manufacture, 59; quoins, 17, 61, 161; regulation, 42; rubbed, 44; rubbers, 47; 'stocks', 47; tax, 8–9, 61
Bricklayers' Guild, 44
Bridgewater, Duke of, 153
Brighton, 109, 147
Buckingham Palace, 61, 101, 109
Buckinghamshire, 118, 132
bugs, bed, 100–1
builders, 26–33, 36–7, 59–63
building: agreement, 34; firm, 37; plot, 34
Bunney, Michael, 163
Burton, Mrs, 93–4, 100, 114, 126
Bury St Edmunds, 8, 86
Byng, John, 15, 101, 142

Cambridgeshire, 73
Campbell, Colen, 5, 30
candles, 93–4, 96
Canonbury Place, 165
canopies, 17–18
Canterbury, 8
Carlyle, Jane and Thomas, 50–2
carpets, 88, 90
Carron Foundry, 127
casements: metal, 116, 136; wooden, 112
Castle of Otranto, 135
categories, house, 12–24, 32, 42
Catterick, 82
ceilings, 17, 22, 82
cellars, 15, 42
cesspits, 42, 105–6
Chalkin, 62
Chambers, Sir William, 22, 132
chandelier, 94
Charlton Mackrell rectory, 138
Chatsworth, 93, 113, 119
Chelsea, 50–2; Hospital, 44
Cheltenham, 15
Cheshire, 153
Cheyne Row, 50–2
Chichester, 8
chimney: breast, 19; piece, 17, 92–3, 123–5; pot, 122; stack, 16–17, 19, 65, 93
Chimney Pots and Stacks, 122
china, as ornament, 92–3
Chinese architecture, 132, 134
Chinoiserie, 132
Chippendale, Thomas, 132

Chippenham, 73
Chorlton Row, 34
Chalkin, C. W., 26–7, 34, 37
City and Country Workman's Treasury of Design, The, 31
Clandestine Marriage, The, 93
classicism, 17, 23, 48, 123–5, 130–1, 163–7
clay, 9–10, 60
Clean and Decent, 100, 106
cleanliness, 100–2, 108
Clifton, 147
Clifton-Taylor, Alec, 116, 119
Colchester, 32
Cole, Rev. William, 15, 118, 132
Colemore Estate, 26
columns: fireplace, 123–4; furniture, 99; porch, 17, 19–20, 146, 148
Combe, William, 101
Combe Florey, 26, 82
comfort, 4
commode, 102
Connoisseur, 15
Constable, John, 122
conveniences, public, 105
Cooke, Andrew, 101
Corinthian order, 17, 20
Cork, Lord, 15
corner stones, 14
Cornforth, John, 165
cornice: Regency, 149, 151; wooden, 14, 17, 19, 44
cottage: classical, 160; farm, 70–2; ornée, 141–2; records, 161
country houses, 9–10, 131, 133
Coventry, Duchess of, 100
Cowes, 139
Cowper, William, 80, 132, 141
craftsmen, 26–31, 86, 90, 99
Cranmer, Archbishop, 78
crime, 53–4
Cruikshank, Dan, 31, 115
Cubitt, Thomas, 36–7
curtains, 79, 88, 90, 99

dado, 23, 51, 86
dating houses, 11–24
Dedham, 9
Deeley, Josiah, 27
Defoe, Daniel, 69, 92
depression, housing, 34
Derbyshire, 114
design, 31

Designs of Chinese Buildings, 132
Designs for Villas, 115
developers, land, 34–7
Development of English Building Construction, The, 46
Devon, 105
dining room, 86–7, 89, 92
disease, 106–7, 110
disguise, architectural, 146–7
documents, 153–61
door, front: Adam, 22; canopied, 17–18; columns, 17, 19–20, 29, 146, 148; panelled, 19; pedimented, 20; steps, 16; vista beyond, 5
Doric order, 17, 146, 148
dormers, 15, 17
Dorset, 82
Downe, Lord, 100
Downing, A. J., 73–5
Downing Street, 165
drawing room, 91–2
Drury Lane, 53

Early Georgian (1720–50): bedroom, 99–100; doorcase, 19–20; farmhouse, 69–70; fireplace, 125; house, 19–20; window, 114
Eassie, W., 106
East Sutton, 156
economy in building, 59–63
Edinburgh, 105
elegance, 10
Enclosure, 78
Encyclopaedia of Cottage, Villa and Farm Architecture, 97, 151
England in the Eighteenth Century, 69
English Domestic Architecture, 163
English Furniture Styles, 90
English Parsonage, The, 84
entablature, 151
Epsom, 99
Erith, Raymond, 165–7
Essex, 5, 9, 32, 154
Exeter, 105

farm: house, 65–75; maps, 154; workers, 70–2
farming, and parsons, 77, 84
Fastnedge, Ralph, 90
ferme ornée, 10, 141
Fersfield, 82

Field, Horace, 163
Fielding, Henry, 46, 54, 118
Fiennes, Celia, 99, 114
Filmer, Sir Edward, 156
fire: danger, 17, 46–7; domestic, 94, 96
Fire, Great, 42–3
fireplace, 22
firescreen, 127
Fitzroy Square, 122
Flemish bond, 8, 44, 61, 63
Fletcher, Rev. Valentine, 122
floor construction, 60
Foots Cray rectory, 159
Foston-le-Clay, 81
Foreign View of England, A, 108
Foundling Hospital, 62
France, glassmakers from, 116
frieze, 151
front, house, 8–9, 20, 23, 44, 48, 61, 63, 148
furniture: bedroom, 99–103, 124; Chinese, 132; dining room, 86–7, 89, 92; drawing room, 91–2; Gothic, 97, 132; probate inventory, 155, 158–9

gable, brick, 71
garden, 5, 32, 105
Gately Park, 166
Gentleman and Cabinet-maker's Director, The, 132
George III, 65, 122
George IV, 109
Georgian Group, 167
Georgian London, 42
Georgian revival, 163
Georgians at Home, The, 93
Geree, Rev. John, 82
Gibson Square, 165
Gillray, 89
glass: manufacture, 21, 116, 118; mirror, 86, 88, 92; sheet, 118–20
glebe: house, 159; land, 77–8, 80; terriers, 154, 157–8
Gloag, John, 117
Gloucestershire, 15
Goede, 65
Gothic: decoration, 149; fireplace, 124, 132; furniture, 97; houses, 130–9; novel, 135; parsonage, 84, 136–9; villas, 145
government, local, 41, 109–10

grate, hob, 127–8
Great Ormond Street, 42, 44
Greater London Council, 41
Greek architecture, 135, 146, 148, 151
Grosvenor Estate, 36
Guestling, 80
Guilds, 44
gutters, 14

Hadlow, 158
Halfpenny, William, 77
Ham, Elizabeth, 82
Hampshire, 37
Hampstead, 147
Hampton Court, 113
Harden, John, 94–6
hardwood, 60
Harvey, John, 153
Hatton, 82
Haworth, 80
Hellyer, S. A., 105, 107
Hepplewhite, 102
Herefordshire, 80, 166
Hervey, Lord, 102
Hints for Dwellings, 141
Historical Monuments Commission, 153
Hobson, John, 114
Holkham, 107
Holland, Henry, 10
Holland, windows 46, 113
Holme, Thea, 50, 52
Horsley, Dr, 84
Hospital: Chelsea, 44; Foundling, 62; London, 109; St George's, 108–9
Howitt, William, 69, 144–5
Hull, 27, 39
Hunmanby, 82
Hunt, Leigh, 51–2
hygiene, 105–9

immigrant skill, 116
improvement, house, 112–20, 130–9, 155–9
incumbency, 78, 154
Innocent, C. F., 46
inns, 101
investment, 37
Ionic order, 17, 20, 148
Ireland, 12
Italy, 7, 45, 141

Jekyll, Rev. George, 82–3
Jenkins, Simon, 35
Johnson, Madame, 100
Johnson, Samuel, 4, 114
joists, timber, 60, 71
Jones, Inigo, 42, 116
Journal of a Tour, 55

Kalm, Pehr, 68
Kedleston, 107
Kent, 8–9, 78, 155–61
Kent, William, 107, 130
Kentish Gazette, 47, 154
Kentish rubbers, 47
Kenwood, 22
King's School shop, 8
Kirle family, 79
kitchen: basement, 15–16; condition, 88, 90, 108; fireplace, 127–8
Knowles, John, 50

Laing, David, 141
Lake District, 67, 94
lamps, 94, 97
Lancashire, 27, 34, 37
landlords, 34–9
Langley, Batty, 31, 130
Late Georgian (1780–1810): doorcase, 23, 28; economy in building, 60–3; farmhouse, 74, 81–3; fireplace, 127; house, 22–4; window, 113, 117
Lauderdale, Duke of, 113
Le Blanc, Jean, 68
Letcombe, 82
Letters on the English and French Nations, 68
Lewes, 8
lighting, 93–7
Lincoln's Inn Fields, 42
Lindsey House, 42
Liverpool, 37
London: building material, 59–63; chimneys, 122; façades, 20; living, 50–7; neo-classicism, 164–5; Regency, 148, 151; sanitation, 101, 109; semi-detached, 147; specific buildings, 22, 35–7, 42–4, 50, 53, 61–2, 101, 109, 113, 146–7, 164; speculative building, 29–32; squares, 35–7, 57; suburbia, 147; terraces, 41–7; water supply, 108

London: the Art of Georgian Building,
  31
London Gazette, 116
lottery, government, 36
Loudon, J. C., 68, 97
Lucas, Dr, 108
luxury, rural, 68–9

Macaulay, Thomas Babington, 82
Machines at Home, 94
mahogany, 90, 92
Maidstone, 155
Malet, Hugh, 153
Malton, James, 115
Manchester, 27
manners, 68
Mansion House, 109
mansions, 4–5, 47
maps, 155–6
marble: artificial, 126–7; bath, 109;
  fireplace, 126–8
Margate, 154
mass-production, 22
matches, 97
Mayhew, Henry, 101
Mechanick Exercises, 44
Mélanges sur l'Angleterre, 88
Mid Georgian (1750–85): bedroom,
  100; cottages, 70–3; doorcase, 21;
  fireplace, 126; furniture, 90–1;
  house, 9, 20–1; parsonage, 78–80
middle class, 2–4
Middlesex, 78
mirrors, 86, 88, 92
modernization, 163–5
modillions, 14, 148
Mohocks gang, 54
mortar, 59–60, 62
motifs, Adam, 38
mouldings, 22, 38, 124–5
Moxon, Joseph, 44
Much Marcle, 79
mud, 9–10, 60

Nash, John, 61, 141, 146
neatness, 10
Nettlestead Rectory, 158
Newbury, 138
Newcastle, Duke of, 34
newspapers, as sources, 153–4
noise, 51–5
Norfolk, 36, 67–8, 77, 80
North, Roger, 42

Nottingham, 27, 34–5

oak, 92
Observer's Book of Furniture, 100
order, 56
Orford, Lord, 73
ornaments, 22–3, 92–3
Osterley, 107

Pain, William, 29
Palazzo Antonini, 7
Palladian: houses, 4–12, 23, 30, 42,
  47–8, 122; parsonages, 78, 80–2;
  villas, 141
Palladio, Andrea, 4, 7, 10, 30, 122,
  165, 167
Palmer, Robert, 35
panelling, 17, 19, 21, 50–1, 92
Panier Close, 27
Papworth, John, 136–7
parapet, 19, 46
parlour, 16, 74–5, 77, 90–3
Parr, Rev. Samuel, 82
parsonage, 77–84, 136–7, 157–9
parsons, 77–84
pediment, central, 7, 14, 16, 67
perukes, 69
Phillips, Dr Daniell, 79
Picturesque, cult of, 134, 141
pilasters, 17–20, 149
Pilcher, Donald, 88
Pimlico, 36
pisé de terre, 9–10, 133
Pitzhanger, 88
plague, 72
plans: Chinese, 132; cottage, 160;
  country house, 131, 133;
  farmhouse, 69, 72, 74; house,
  12–14; improvements, 154–8;
  parsonage, 77, 136–9; Regency,
  151; terrace, 41, 47; villa, 115
Plans for Cottages . . . of the Labourer,
  72, 160
Plaw, John, 10, 131, 133
Plumb, J. H., 69, 109
plumbing, 105, 109
police, 54
ponds, 15
portico, 7, 14, 67, 145
Portsmouth, 37
pot, chamber, 102–3, 105
Practical Home Carpenter, The, 29
Prince Albert, 106

privy, 105–6
probate inventories, 155, 158–9
prosperity, rural, 68–9
Provincial Towns of England, The, 26
Purefoy, Elizabeth and Henry, 91,
    126–7

Quattro Libri dell'Architettura, 4, 7,
    141, 165
Queen Anne period (1700–20):
    bedroom, 99; fireplace, 124; front
    door, 18; furniture, 91–2; houses,
    14, 16–19; mansions, 47; roofs,
    14; terraces, 47, 50
Queen Anne's Bounty, 77, 159
Queen Mary, 92
Queen Victoria, 109, 138
quoins, 17, 61, 161

Reeve, Clara, 135
Regency period (1800–30): dainty,
    151; doorcase, 146; farmhouse,
    83–4; fireplace, 128; furniture,
    86–8, 95–6; Gothic, 137; houses,
    148–51; portico, 145; roof, 148;
    rural life, 144–5; villas, 145–7;
    windows, 115
Regency Style, The, 88
Regent's Park, 61, 146
Renaissance influence, 12, 65, 67,
    116
rent: ground, 39, 62; peppercorn,
    29–30
restrictions, building, 34–5, 57, 60
Robins, Thomas, 134
Rochefoucauld, François de la, 86,
    88, 108, 117
Rochester, 157
Romano, Giulio, 45
roof: Queen Anne, 14; Regency,
    148; rooms in, 12, 15; tiled, 17,
    46; truncated, 12, 14–15, 17
Rowlandson, pictures, 79, 81, 83
Royal Academy, 165
Royal Crescent, 72
Royal Lodge, 165
rubbers, 47
rubbish, 59–60, 105
Rumford stone, 128
rural life, 65–75, 144–5
Rural Life in England, 69, 144
Rural Residences, 136–7
Russell Square, 37

safety, 54–5
St Albans, Duke of, 36
Sanditon, 143
sanitation, 105–9
Saussure, César de, 108
Scotland, 105, 127
Scott, Dr Alexander, 82
Scott, Sir Walter, 136
scullery, 141
Selling parish, 156
semi-detached, 72–3, 147
servants, 50–1, 68, 70–2, 88
sewage, 105–6, 109–10
shafts, 149
Shepperton Rectory, 78
Sheraton, 86, 102
shops, 116–17
Simond, Louis, 55, 60, 110, 139, 143
sites, for villas, 142–4
Sketches for Country Houses, 131, 133
skill, lack of, 43–4
Smith, Rev. Sydney, 26, 81–2
Smollett, Tobias, 105
social conditions, 67–8
softwood, 60, 62
Somerset, 26, 34, 72, 91, 138–9
Somerset House, 132
sources, historical, 153–61
Southall, Mary, 101
Sparham, 80
speculation, building, 29–31, 61
Spencer, Lady Sarah, 4
stairs: balusters, 4, 21, 50; carved,
    50; convenient, 4, 6; dog-leg, 16;
    farmhouse, 65; Palladian, 6
Stamford, 130
standardization of building, 32
Sterne, Laurence, 114
Stourhead, 130
stone, 8–9, 128
stove, 127–8
Stranger in England, The, 65
Strawberry Hill, 132, 134–5
streets, 51–5
Stuart houses, 116, 122
stucco, 23, 61, 147, 149
study, 77, 82–3
Stukeley, Rev. William, 130
suburbia, 145–7
Suffolk, 8, 86
summer houses, 130, 134
Summerson, Sir John, 12, 30, 42,
    135, 146

Sussex, 8, 80, 109
Swift, Jonathan, 54, 105
symmetry, 2–4, 15–16, 42, 75
Syon House, 107

Task, The, 80
tax: brick, 8–9, 61; window, 117–18
tea, 108
Tenterden, 9
terraces: categories, 16; first, 41–8;
    interior description, 55–6; new,
    163; symmetry, 15–16, 42; villa,
    146
Terry, Quinlan, 165, 167
Thompson, Benjamin, 128
Tiffin & Son, 101
tiles, mathematical, 8
timber supports, 60, 62
Tite Street, 50
tithes, 78, 81, 84
Tom Jones, 118
Torrington Diaries, 143
Torrington Square, 37
trade, forbidden, 35
Tristram Shandy, 114
Tunbridge Wells, 9
Twickenham, 132, 134
typhus, 106, 110

Vicar of Wakefield, The, 80–1
Victorian influence, 50, 119, 122,
    142, 151
villa, 141–8
Vitruvius Britannicus, 30

Waistell, Charles, 70
Walker, John, 97
walnut, 90–2
walls, exterior: brick, 8–9, 20, 46,
    61; façade, 8–9, 44, 48; painted,
    147; stucco, 23, 61, 147, 149;
    supports, 62; thickness, 47;
    weatherboarding, 61
walls, interior: Adam, 21–4; colour
    washed, 21, 23–4; curved, 24;
    dado, 23, 51, 86; frieze, 22;
    panelled, 17, 19, 21, 50–1; party,
    31, 60
Walpole, Horace, 4, 100, 132, 134–5
Warde, Parson, 78
Ware, Isaac, 31, 77, 107, 123
Wars, Napoleonic, 60, 141
Warwickshire, 26–7, 37, 62, 82

water closets, 107, 110
water: heating, 128; supply, 56–7,
    106–10
Waters, An Essay on, 108
Watkinson, William, 94
weatherboarding, 61
Wells cathedral, 139
West Coker, 82
Weston Longville, 77
Weston-under-Penyard, 79
Weymouth, 147
Whitehall, Banqueting Hall, 113
Whitehead, William, 132
wigs, 56, 69, 81, 101–2
Wild, Jonathan, 54
Wilde, Oscar, 50
William III, 92
William IV, 113
Wiltshire, 73
windows: Adam, 22–3; arches, 47;
    bay, 149; blocked, 118; casement,
    17, 46, 112, 115–16, 136, 149;
    direction, 72; dormer, 17, 79, 115;
    farmhouse, 65; glass, 21, 116–20;
    Gothic, 113, 136; hinged, 112;
    mullioned, 112, 136; sash, 17, 20,
    23, 46, 79, 112–20, 148; shop,
    116–17; shuttered, 32, 46–7; size,
    20–1; tax, 117–18; triple, 23;
    Venetian, 6, 23
Windsor, 134, 165
Windsor Castle, 106, 113
Windsor rubbers, 47
Woburn, 10
Woburn Square, 37
Wood, John, junior, 72, 132, 160
Wood, John, senior, 99
Woodforde, Rev. James, 77–8, 80–1,
    102, 105
Woodside, 134
Wookey rectory, 139
workers, farm, 70–2
Works in Architecture, 22
Worthing, 147
Wotton, Sir Henry, 124
Wrangham, Rev. Francis, 82
Wren, Sir Christopher, 44, 51, 124, 130
Wright, Lawrence, 100, 106, 109

Yalding, 78
York Terrace, 146
Yorkshire, 27, 80–2, 114
Young Woman's Companion, The, 100